LIMINAL PEOPLE

TERRIFYING NIGHTMARE PARALLEL REALITIES

G. MICHAEL VASEY

Copyright © 2022 by G. Michael Vasey

Published by Raven Tale Publishing

All rights reserved. No part of this publication may be reproduced, stored in a retrieval system or transmitted, in any form, or by any means, electronic, mechanical, recorded, photocopied, or otherwise, without the prior written permission of both the copyright owner and the above-mentioned publisher of this book, except by a reviewer who may quote brief passages in a review.

The scanning, uploading, and distribution of this book via the Internet or via any other means without the permission of the publisher is illegal and punishable by law. Please purchase only authorized electronic editions and do not participate in or encourage electronic piracy of copyrighted materials.

This is a work of fiction. Names, characters, places and incidents either are a product of the author's imagination or are used fictitiously, and any resemblance to actual persons, living or dead, business establishments, events, or locales is purely coincidental unless used to add historical perspective.

ISBN: 9798821781703

Created with Vellum

1
INTRODUCTION

Most of my life, I have had an interest in the paranormal, which was really forced on me due to my innate psychism and a childhood[1] filled with ghosts, poltergeist, and other weird experiences. At an early age, I also developed an interest in the occult and magic and read avidly anything I could get my hands on, from the lurid occult novels of Dennis Wheatley to the magical books by Crowley and others. Meanwhile, I studied geology to Ph.D. level at college and soon became intrigued by quantum physics as well. This strange mix was probably behind my first novella, *The Last Observer*[2], and its tale of magic, quantum worlds, and good and evil.

For the last ten years, I have collected stories of the paranormal—true accounts of others' real experiences—and now have thousands of them at my disposal. You can leave me yours too if you wish at the *My Haunted Life Too* website[3]. I have continued to pursue my interests in magic and in dowsing and geobiology. Over the last few years, I have used a combination of my own knowledge and experience, these stories, and basic research to write a series of short books on everything from poltergeists to the Black-Eyed Kids and much in between. Often, these books started with a personal experience or an account that someone sent me that piqued my interest. This book also comes of a personal experience as you shall see.

Over the years, I have concluded that all is not what it appears to be. I took the red pill back in my teens and have been wide awake quite a bit of my life, watching how our world and reality is manufactured for us by whoever are the earthly powers. I am convinced that whoever they are, they know much they are not telling as they use methods and tools against us all that would otherwise be termed black magic.

However, one should maintain an open mind and not fall for their politicized science story. Science is never proven. Science is the creation of hypotheses and a raucous debate over them until a new hypothesis emerges. Besides, when materialists argue against paranormal and magical effects, they deny science (look up the placebo effect for example) and certainly show their ignorance of the quantum world. Everything you take as fact is actually probably a lie. History in particular is suspect in many ways even in terms of the origins of humanity and the existence of ancient technologies and civilizations.

I think that what I am about to discuss in this book is known and has been known throughout human history. That is that there are other entities and beings that share the space we live in. They live in parallel worlds in a way, and some are aware of our existence as well. Some of you would call them angelic and others, demonic. Some exist on the very edge of our perception. These are the liminal people.

2

LIMINAL PEOPLE

Liminal People?

What on earth does liminal mean anyway? Liminal means out on the edge or boundary. It means that in-between place that is neither quite here nor there. A transitional place between here and there, perhaps. Or according to one definition that I found, *"occupying a position at or on both sides of a boundary or threshold."* I sometimes call them peripheral people as well, as they are on the periphery of our reality and theirs. We see them and interact when some set of circumstances, often purely by chance, push us into that liminal world out there on the edge of our reality.

I have experienced liminal people and beings much of my life, but it was only when I started dowsing earth energies that I started to understand what this phenomenon was and just how all-encompassing the idea of liminal people could be.

Out dowsing earth energy lines one afternoon here in Brno, Czechia, I saw a couple of interesting characters that seemed to do disappearing acts unexpectedly. Unsure of what I had encountered, if anything at all, I made a short video[1] and called these people *peripheral people*. I asked those who watched the video if they had ever experienced anything similar, and several of them left comments or wrote to me saying that they had. My interest in whatever this might be was born.

I had been walking with my dowsing rods up a long straight road on an incline just north of Brno. When dowsing, I am in a different state of consciousness—almost meditating—with an empty mind. There were quite a few folks about as in the town below as there was an autumn festival and fair going on. I was tracking a twelve-metre-thick energy line up the hill. As I was walking, I noticed an old lady. What attracted my attention was the incongruency of her appearance, actions, and location. She sat on a small fold-up stool by the side of a hedge that surrounded a large house. She had numerous bags stuffed with what I thought were groceries. She paid me no attention as she was engrossed in looking for something under the hedge with one arm—or so I thought. She looked like an ordinary old person. Gray hair, slightly old-fashioned shoes and clothing. For a second, I pondered if she were homeless.

I continued to walk up the road, soon losing sight of the

old lady. I found the energy line and marked it on the application on my phone and then decided to walk back and ensure that I could find the line again—this is my method of checking that it is a line and not a spurious response from the rods I use. I noted again the old lady, still sweeping her hand under the base of the hedge and into the back garden of the house. I wondered what she might be looking for. She paid me no attention at all.

I then turned and started back up the hill, finding the line again and confirming it was there. At that point, I was going back to my car to drive a while to pick up the line on another road, and so I set off back down the hill watching the people below at the fair. As I walked past the old lady's location, I looked over. There was no one there! I was a bit surprised, and so, I looked all around. No sign of any lady, bags, or folding stool anywhere. I spent several minutes looking and searching for her. An old lady with a stool and many bags simply could not have got very far, yet she had vanished.

I thought this a little odd. How could this lady, who looked to be around 80, have gotten up and left with all those full plastic bags and her seat and gotten so far away as to not be visible in a minute or less? As I walked to my car, I kept half an eye out for her but saw nothing.

As I drove into Brno later in the day, I was thinking what a strange day it had been anyway. Sometimes, when working with these earth energy lines, strange coincidences happen. This had been one such day, filled with small bird feathers on the lines, involving me parking my car randomly only to discover I had parked on the line I was looking for, and then, there was that old lady!

I pulled up into the only parking spot on the road and got out. I was looking to pick up another line that I had previously mapped to a certain point. I soon found that I had again managed to park my car on it! I shook my head in disbelief at yet another strange coincidence. I followed the line, which was marked with small white bird feathers everywhere. I tracked it into an abandoned factory site. There were numerous lockups there, now used garages or storage.

As I was dowsing the line and marking it on the phone application, I noticed an old man. What drew my attention to him was that he looked just like Santa but without the red clothes. Big white bushy hair and whiskers, he was tubby, too and sat against a lockup door. I immediately thought him a homeless man and continued my dowsing work. Again, somehow this man looked odd. Out of place. So, I glanced up to have another look. Nothing! He was gone. This time, I did a longer search, all the while talking to myself under my breath that I was indeed losing my sanity. There was no one around and no Santa-like man anywhere to be seen.

That was the end of my day. Too much weirdness. I got in the car and drove home, and I made the video wondering if others had had similar weird experiences with these peripheral people. I even Googled the term I had coined but found nothing of value. However, I came to a couple of possible explanations. Either this was just a case of being focused on some activity so intently that I failed to notice these people leave, or these people were living in the edge of our reality somehow. Either way, this was an interesting phenomenon. What struck me was the incongruity of the two people. They were just weirdly out of place as if they did not belong.

I posted the video and wrote a blog post asking for other stories or ideas around the phenomenon that I was describing and was quite surprised at the number of comments and emails that I received in reply. It seemed that 'peripheral people' were something that others had also experienced and in many different forms and situations. I then started combing the Internet for additional stories and encounters of this type and found many examples.

So, what are 'peripheral people?' When I first started to research them, I was unsure. Was this a paranormal experience? Or was it simply something to do with people's perception of time and events? Either way, I deemed it a fascinating study and set about investigating it further in the hope of arriving at a satisfactory explanation.

First, however, what are "peripheral people?"

For me, these are people on the edge of reality. They are liminal people who may belong to this reality or to another that overlaps with it. They look odd and out of place—incongruent with the environment in which they are observed. They are transitory; there one minute and gone without trace the next. They can be helpful, intervening in moments of danger and adversity, and they can be menacing, threatening, and scary, and that appears to be deliberate and designed to elicit a fear response. They can also be apparently inconsequential, not interacting at all but rather simply present in the background in an odd, unrelated sort of way and then gone in an instant. Sometimes, they may be paranormal entities, and other times they maybe ordinary people caught in an odd moment of attention and focus or perhaps something in between. Whether they are of another reality or this one, for the observer, they are on the periphery or liminal edge of reality.

Let's get a sense of what these people are by examining a few encounter stories. First, when I posted the video and blog talking about my encounters, I received quite a lot of replies in which others explained their experiences. Here are a few examples.

When I was in my late 20s and single, about 5 or 6 years ago, I went on a pubcrawl with some friends, and we had a good time and got drunk. It was wintertime, and on my way home I slipped and fell on the cobble stones. I bashed my head on the ground, but I got up quickly. Nobody saw me, and I stumbled on home.

When I got there about 10 minutes later, I discovered I had lost my keys. It was about 3am in the morning, and panic kicked in. I searched the cobblestone road, went back to some of the cafés without success. I went on looking around the place I fell for 5 or 10 minutes without any result. Tired and intoxicated, I sat myself down against a building and called some of my friends (of course, no one answered at 4:30ish). I felt like a homeless person and decided to go to the station for some warmth and call my landlady at 9am for the spare keys.

As I got up a man across the empty street (who looked a bit like me, only 10 years older and very thin, like a junky) yelled at me, ' you will be all right man!' Shaking my head, I replied, 'Who?! Me?' 'Yeah, you!' I thought it was some nutjob and headed towards the station. Maybe 5 or 6 steps later I saw my keys on the ground. I couldnt believe it. I wanted to say to the man across the street he was right, but as you can guess, he was gone, and I never saw him again. I feel like it was me from another time and place. Or maybe it was just a crazy junky.

On a holiday in England, my father was making a sketch in a church. We were outside playing in the churchyard, and he came out saying that a man had appeared for a chat and then disappeared.

I saw a car heading towards me a short distance away on a long straight road, which caused me to reconsider the overtaking manoeuvre I was about to execute. I pulled in, and when I looked again it (within a second or two) had vanished. There was no turning for it to vanish into, and this was a wide-open road in the Cambridgeshire Fens with a flat, open vista.

A few seconds later when I passed the part of the road where it had disappeared, there was nothing to see. It hadn't driven into the roadside large open drain (manmade river); it had simply disappeared. I was left with the distinct feeling that this apparition was designed to slow me down (I used to hurtle along those Fen roads despite the dangers of the roadside drains that had taken the lives of a few over the years), and that this whole experience was a blessing to keep me safe.

Many years ago, I had a friend that was on vacation and got lost in a bad neighborhood in a city. Sorry I don't remember the city. She sat at a bus stop to catch a bus hoping to get out of there. Then, out of nowhere, a large black woman with many shopping bags was sitting next to her. The black woman told her not to get on the bus and pointed to a bus stop where she should catch a bus. My friend was looking where the bag lady was pointing, and then she looked back at her to thank her, but she was gone. She figured it may have been an angel because there's no way the woman could have left without a sound with all those shopping bags.

Very interesting! I know of stories like that and think I experienced this—saw a dude walking down the street. I was at my balcony, and when he passed under it, he disapeared. I even checked the road on both sides.

I was walking with a group of seven for a camping location in the mendip hills in the middle of nowhere, and we passed a house or cottage, which the window caught my attention. There was an old woman stitching by the last light of the day at the window. With me being the straggler of the group, I called out to those nearest to me, "Aah look how cool that is, real ritual working by that old woman," turning with those wanting to look she'd disappeared! You dont take it in as much when out of breath doing a long walk, but when remembering back in a conversation with one who was on that trip, he also acknowledges he'd seen her and was also surprised by her disappearence. This was in Devon.

One or two wrote emails to me, and one kind gentlemen took the trouble to write an account of his experience. Here is Chris Inman's account in his own words (thank you so much!).

Background

I've never felt like I was from here and always felt like I was observing mankind's interactions. Growing up, I seemed to gravitate towards people who were picked on or manipulated by other stronger, less empathetic people. It wasn't until I was married that I sorted out a healing technique to help my wife with her migraine attacks. At this time I was drawn to Reiki healing, which I trained in over three years. Since then I've researched Eastern mystical practices such as Daoism and Buddhism as well as different Shamanic teachings. After completing my Reiki training, I attended a local development circle for two years training in mediumship. One night we did a meditation to gain guidance. I found myself surrounded by a council of elders so I asked, "Why are we here?" I was told there will be a coming worldwide event that will turn this reality on its head and that we are here as aid workers and healers to support those who can't assimilate with the new reality.

I waited for 16 years building on my knowledge and Reiki practice with the help and support of the only person who understands where I'm coming from, my Reiki Master. Then, March last year we were put into lockdown, and I knew that this was the beginning of what was to come. I've spent the last 18 months watching it all unfold looking for signs. The more this carries on, the more I've disconnected from the mind of the masses and await the tipping point.

My psychic abilities revolve around what I call the Daydream part of my mind where I receive images as well as thoughts. In all my years I have never seen before me a visualisation of guides or helpers, so I tend to think all the messages and guidance I have received come from my higher self/daemon. This is what makes what happened more relevant than ever.

My Experience

It was a clear sunny morning on 7th September 2021. My wife and I had decided to take out our one-year-old granddaughter for the day as the following day we were going away for four days, and she was going to Spain for a week with her parents on the day we returned home.

We decided to take her for a walk around the grounds of Temple Newsam in Leeds, a stately home with past associations with knight templars. The reason we decided on it was the years of dog walks we have done there. We arrived at midday, and it didn't seem too busy as we parked up at the north end of the estate. We took our usual route that leads through a small wooded area, down the hill to three duck ponds that lay at the bottom of the valley.

As we approached the second, larger pond, my granddaughter became mesmerized by the ducks on the pond so we stood with the pushchair on the bank to watch them. As we prepared to move on, between the trees to the lower pond, something caught my eye. I looked up the hill towards the main house where a path leads back down the hill to the ponds. What I saw was a figure dressed in Lycra below-the-knee exercise leggings, trainers, and a fitness crop top, carrying a bottle of water. As I looked my brain went into overdrive, my eyes saw what I thought was a feminine figure with what seemed like a masculine physique. Not a bodybuilder's physique but more like what you would expect of what I can only describe as a Valkyrie, Norse shield maiden, or, if you're old enough, Xena warrior princess. I diverted my eyes as I thought if I stare too long I might get grief from my wife, although I must state implicitly there was no physical attraction on my behalf.

We continued to the last pond in that the route we would normally take back up to the house was blocked off by fencing due to an upcoming food festival. We decided to proceed along the path that leads farther down the valley. After about 100 metres we sat on a small bridge over a stream to rest in the shade. We set off back, and I noticed a couple in their teens walking farther in front of us.

As we came back to the last pond, I looked up; there she/it was walking towards us. It felt like I was in a glass tunnel between us, and everything outside of the tunnel was muffled and blurred, like tunnel vision. She passed a woman sat on a bench who didn't bat an eye in her direction, which I found odd, and the teen male from the couple did the same, which I found strange; I was sure she would have caught his eye. All the time I couldn't look away. She had mousey blonde shoulder-length straight hair that reminded me of a spartan helmet, she seemed under-stylised for a woman with a perfect physique. She also wasn't wearing makeup and didn't need it. Close up, she had a squared jaw with a broad face, yet everything about her seemed perfect. As we got closer to each other we never broke eye contact, and all I could hear in my mind was "You see me!!" repeating over and over. Her expression, I'd describe as enigmatic like the Mona Lisa, which never changed through the whole experience. The closer we got the more awkward I felt so when we were within arm's length I muttered "Hi" and smiled as she carried on past me. I didn't look back as I thought my wife would have clocked on to what was going on and might have had some choice words for me. The rest of the day was uneventful, and I spent much of it scratching my head in a daze.

Afterword

The following day we went away to Whitby, and for the following four days as we walked through the crowds I felt no connection to the people around us. As I replayed the experience in my mind I felt like I knew her from another reality, and we came from the same place. I spent the rest of the holiday trying to see another one but to no avail.

On my return I spoke with my friend and Reiki Master who reminded me of your podcast with Thomas Sheridan and wondered if our experiences were the same. Then as if by fate you put up a video on YouTube asking for other people's experiences, and here we are.

I've spent a while to reply as it seems I was putting the puzzle pieces together and hope it is of help to your future venture. Glad to know I'm not alone.

Another person, Nathalie, also took the time to write to me. This is her story.

The last one was a few weeks ago. I met a man, homeless, in the city on my way to the garage parking. This man put a finger on his lips, telling me "shhh..." Smiling away. We shared a "knowing," a knowing of all that is happening around us in the world. He knew I knew and the way around. No words, no conversation. I turned around and gave him some good money, at the same time I felt this wasn't necessary at all. But okay to do anyway. I was sure no one else has seen him, it's this odd feeling known to me...

Another one was years ago when I was a teenager. I was waiting for the train I think or tram (living in the Netherlands), and while waiting a young man approached me, and he asked me some questions about my life but in such a genuine way with interest that I was telling him my whole life story before I realized what I was doing. Even at that time, I was quite astonished how he could make me talk about myself in such a way. But during this meeting, I have had this same odd feeling. And I never forget you know...

I probably have met those kinds of people way more than I realise, but this will be the last one to write about. I was around 10 years old. My parents and I drove back from old Yugoslavia to home, it was early in the morning and we were in Germany on the highway. I was out of my body with my spirit guides, they told me before I went back, be careful by stepping out of the car, you've had an accident and there is glass all over.

And so I came back to my body with the car upside down, and because I knew, I stayed calm. I did panic a bit when I saw my mother stepping out with blood on her face. The next thing I remember I was watching the show so to speak, my mother surrounded by doctors, my father talking to the police. Between the doctors stood another man, long tall blond, with a white doctor's coat, pretending to be a doctor. I could tell straight away, even at that age, he wasn't human-like.

Telepathically he asked me,

"Please, let me help you.

Last time you denied my help.

Please do take it now..."

He was almost begging, and although I was quite okay, I felt sorry for him if I would deny him again, so telepathically I agreed to, and he gave me a big smile and walked over towards me and took my hand.

After this, I don't know what happened, besides sitting in the ambulance. The man and a woman too this time came a bit later again in the hospital to check out if I was alright, this time more mentally instead of physically.

I was also contacted by Amanda from the USA by email who told this story.

My father, Gary, was killed in Vietnam in 1971. Nobody ever told me I didn't have an open line to talk to him, so I did. I always talked to him, asked him questions and received answers. Most of it was just generic stuff, but it came to music, and he'd tell me favorite songs. I inherited his album collection years later and found copies of his faves.

My Mom was to remarry in July 1985. She had dreams that my Dad was there at her wedding. As she was getting the house ready for my Buddy (her second husband who eventually adopted me) to move in, she had out photograph albums to be boxed up and moved to the attic. Buddy came in and flipped through them. He [came] across a photo of my Dad holding me and demanded to know who it was. When Mom told him that was my Father, he said "it can't be, I saw him last week."

Buddy was an engineer and worked on military targets and aircraft. He'd been at Pensacola Air Base in Pensacola, Florida. My Father is buried at Barrancos National Cemetery on that Air Base because he was born in Florida.

As my Buddy told the story he said he saw a man smiling at him as he approached, and then he winked just before he passed by. When Buddy turned to look, the man was gone. We all felt certain that my Dad was giving his blessing.

In 2014 my brother passed, then my son in 2015. In 2018 I lost Buddy, but he went and returned. He passed on 7/10 in the hospital, but my uncle walked in, not knowing what was happening and ran a cold soda across my Buddy's exposed stomach. Buddy sat up with a deep breath. An hour later he was more himself, and he said, "Mandy, the lines are all busy, but I saw Xander. (My son) Xander is here and he's alive!"

Buddy was sent home on Hospice. He passed three days later at home. He had always been afraid to die in a hospital. It struck me that the 3 days later was meaningful—an inverse of Christ's resurrection.

Plainly, a rather mixed lot of different experiences, yet in there are several mentions of realities and what seem like perceived mental connections. So, what is going on here? I decided to hunt through my ghost story submission website to see what I could find in it and soon found some similar type stories that had been submitted there. For example:

One afternoon in 2003, my 8-year-old daughter was playing with her dolls out on our front porch when suddenly a young girl around the age of 15 years old was standing in front of her. My daughter looked up, asked her what she wanted, and the girl replied, "I want you to come with me to a place where it is much more fun than here." Then my daughter Denielle realized she was a stranger and had no way of getting to our front porch because she would need to go through the front gate which is always locked for security reasons. Then she looked at the girl's feet and saw that she was floating about 6 inches from the ground. Scared, she said no and stood up to run into the house through the front door. The stranger grabbed my daughter's arm and tried pulling her away from the front door when my daughter Denielle, with force, got away from her grasp. When she ran into the house she suddenly stopped when seeing her younger siblings and myself sitting on the sofa reading a book.

I asked her what was wrong and she said nothing, but I could see the terror in her eyes. I asked her again and said it is ok to tell mommy. Then she told me what happened. My reply was, "Denielle, don't make up a story like that, you are scaring your sisters." Then she said with an adamant tone, "I'm not making up a story, Mom. Look!" She showed me her arm and there was a faint bruise-like figure of a hand on her arm like someone grabbing it and pulling hard.

To this day we don't know who that young girl might be, and she never again appeared to Denielle.

Submitted by Loiusa Munoz

This took place one summer several years ago. We were in the back yard. My mother was sitting in a chair to my left and dad was sitting to the right, I was in the middle with my favorite blanket. It was a mild day, extremely pleasant—until I looked at the power line running across the backyard.

Now on this power line was a tall man walking in black. The one thing that makes me remember this is the eyes. They were completely black. That feeling when he looked at me though just terrified me. I blinked and he was gone. Nobody else saw him. It was one of the most terrifying things that has ever happened to me. He was standing still on the powerline, he didn't move, he didn't smile. He was just standing there looking at me.

I tried to tell my parents about him—but they thought I was imagining things. In fact, my dad accused me of trying to spoil the day. Mom would listen but she didn't believe me. I spent that whole day wondering who it was, and why he was on the powerlines looking down at me.

Now I have not seen this thing again since that time, but I have experienced quite a bit of weird things. Every time I think about this I can see the eyes perfectly like the first time in my mind staring at me.

Submitted by Neil Shannon, Texas

About five years ago I lived downtown in a major city in the US. I've always been a night person, so I would often find myself bored after my roommate, who was decidedly not a night person, went to sleep. To pass the time, I used to go for long walks and spend the time thinking.

I spent four years like that, walking alone at night and never once had a reason to feel afraid. I always used to joke with my roommate that even the drug dealers in the city were polite. But all of that changed in just a few minutes of one evening.

It was a Wednesday, somewhere between one and two in the morning, and I was walking near a police-patrolled park quite a ways from my apartment. It was a quiet night, even for a week night, with very little traffic and almost no one on foot. The park, as it was most nights, was completely empty.

I turned down a short side street in order to loop back to my apartment when I first noticed him. At the far end of the street, on my side, was the silhouette of a man, dancing. It was a strange dance, similar to a waltz, but he finished each "box" with an odd forward stride. I guess you could say he was dance-walking, headed straight for me.

Deciding he was probably drunk, I stepped as close as I could to the road to give him the majority of the sidewalk to pass me by. The closer he got, the more I realized how gracefully he was moving. He was very tall and lanky and wearing an old suit. He danced closer still, until I could make out his face. His eyes were open wide and wild, head tilted back slightly, looking off at the sky. His mouth was formed in a painfully wide cartoon of a smile. Between the eyes and the smile, I decided to cross the street before he danced any closer.

I took my eyes off of him to cross the empty street. As I reached the other side, I glanced back... and then stopped dead in my tracks. He had stopped dancing and was standing with one foot in the street, perfectly parallel to me. He was facing me but still looking skyward. Smile still wide on his lips.

I was completely and utterly unnerved by this. I started walking again, but kept my eyes on the man. He didn't move.

Once I had put about half a block between us, I turned away from him for a moment to watch the sidewalk in front of me. The street and sidewalk ahead of me were completely empty. Still unnerved, I looked back to where he had been standing to find him gone. For the briefest of moments I felt relieved, until I noticed him. He had crossed the street and was now slightly crouched down. I couldn't tell for sure due to the distance and the shadows, but I was certain he was facing me. I had looked away from him for no more than 10 seconds, so it was clear that he had moved fast.

I was so shocked that I stood there for some time, staring at him. And then he started moving toward me again. He took giant, exaggerated tip-toed steps, as if he were a cartoon character sneaking up on someone. Except he was moving very, very quickly.

I'd like to say at this point I ran away or pulled out my pepper spray or my cellphone or anything at all, but I didn't. I just stood there, completely frozen as the smiling man crept toward me.

And then he stopped again, about a car length away from me. Still smiling his smile, still looking to the sky.

When I finally found my voice, I blurted out the first thing that came to mind. What I meant to ask was, "What the fuck do you want?!" in an angry, commanding tone. What came out was a whimper, "What the fuu...?"

Regardless of whether or not humans can smell fear, they can certainly hear it. I heard it in my own voice, and that only made me more afraid. But he didn't react to it at all. He just stood there, smiling.

And then, after what felt like forever, he turned around, very slowly, and started dance-walking away. Just like that. Not wanting to turn my back to him again, I just watched him go, until he was far enough away to almost be out of sight. And then I realized something. He wasn't moving away anymore, nor was he dancing. I watched in horror as the distant shape of him grew larger and larger. He was coming back my way. And this time he was running.

I ran too.

I ran until I was off of the side road and back onto a better-lit road with sparse traffic. Looking behind me then, he was nowhere to be found. The rest of the way home, I kept glancing over my shoulder, always expecting to see his stupid smile, but he was never there.

I lived in that city for six months after that night, and I never went out for another walk. There was something about his face that always haunted me. He didn't look drunk, he didn't look high. He looked completely and utterly insane. And that's a very, very scary thing to see.

Originally submitted to Reddit

Even more interesting to me, however, were the experiences of my friends, the late Sue Vincent and Stuart France. Sue and Stuart essentially were the ones that got me started with what Sue always called "connecting with the land,"[2] and they documented many of their mystical experiences in a series of books.

It is in *Giant's Dance*[3] that they have a very similar experience to mine, with an old lady with a radiant face and rather disheveled clothing, whom they meet in a church. After talking about her various ailments with a cheerful disposition, she points them to a stained-glass window they should see and then seems to promptly disappear, being nowhere to be seen just a few minutes later. Interestingly, Stuart referred to her as a "quantum person" in email communication recently (see below for the relevance of this). This was not their only interaction with a liminal person, either, as they also later met a man and his dog at a stone circle who also seemed to belong to another world.

Recently, in a podcast interview with me, Thomas Sheridan, Irish artist and magician, related his experiences with a liminal person, who would approach him asking quickfire questions.

So, game on! I wasn't the only one seeing weird people who seemingly disappeared at a moment's notice. It was by all accounts a quite common phenomenon. But what was it? Was it paranormal or just something to do with a momentary lapse in focus?

3

LIMINAL PEOPLE IN THE PARANORMAL WORLD

When I pondered the concept of liminal people, I immediately thought of some of the stories of Black-Eyed people, the hat man, and other shadow people who are often mentioned in the world of the paranormal. It also struck me that on the other side of things were all the stories of angels and the third-man stories in which some mysterious person or entity intervenes in a miraculous way. The more I thought about it, the more I began to find examples of incongruent characters on the edge of reality coming and going in people's lives seemingly at random.

Just recently, I was watching a video interview on YouTube by geobiologist Rory Duff. Rory is the expert on Earth energy lines and vortices, and so, I was intrigued by what he had to say. At one point, he started talking about quantum mechanics and the idea that all dimensions could exist in this one. What he said next rang a chord with me. It was that if everything was vibration and resonance, then what if reality was like an old-fashioned radio dial? An infinite spectrum of frequencies occupied by beings, matter, and consciousnesses operating within discrete bands of vibration. In essence, all these beings could coexist in the same space without ever being aware of the others there because their frequency was too high or low to be detected.

We know that humans can only see, hear, and detect frequencies within a certain range. Dogs and cats have a slightly different range, and perhaps they see and hear things that we do not. So, what if so-called angels were beings of a finer substance and a higher vibration unseen and undetected by us? What if the BEK, shadow people, and the like were denser, lower-vibrational beings also undetected by us? And what if, in certain moments of adjusted consciousness, our detection range expanded a bit?

Think about radio for a while and those days when, due to atmospheric conditions, you can pick up channels that normally would be impossible to listen to. As you listen, you hear on the static, fading in and out, radio stations from the other side of the world or in another band range altogether.

So, now imagine that you are that radio, and normally you detect vibrations within the standard human range, but for some reason that day, that second, your band range is temporarily extended due to some strange atmospheric (or shall we say consciousness) conditions. Perhaps it is deep fear or lust or some unbridled passion that extends your ability to detect lower frequencies momentarily, or perhaps it is meditation or dowsing or listening to music or something that momentarily extends your ability to detect higher frequencies. Suddenly, there are ghostly images and sounds available to you that were not there before. Perhaps liminal people and beings exist not on the edge of reality but simply the edge of our perceived reality.

I could now get into a whole host of quantum mechanics. It is a very strange world and one that I played a little with in my novella, *The Last Observer*. Reality needs an observer to collapse the wave function, meaning that you are constantly observing and creating the reality around you. Furthermore, there is too much information coming in to process so you ignore some of it. Here, there is an aspect of perception and pattern recognition. You perceive what you recognize.

So, if an alien arrived on earth, you may not even perceive it at all as your processor or brain might eliminate the data as it appears unimportant, and it cannot be perceived. Everything you see, hear, and sense occurs inside of your brain and soul. When you look at the page and see the words, you are looking at energy. All matter is energy. What appears solid is in fact empty space—a sort of illusion created by your brain.

Most people have probably never realized that science today postulates that reality is essentially empty space filled with energy. It always makes me laugh when I see or hear people talking about how hard science rules out the paranormal, because it does the reverse—it opens the truly incredible side of reality. You see, once you get into the realms of quantum physics, everything you think you knew about anything evaporates into illusion.

Science sees matter as existing as particles, whether that is the earth (a spherical particle) or an atom or even smaller subatomic particles. However, what we know from the quantum world is that everything exists as waves or vibrations. The universe is space filled with energy in the form of waves or vibrations, and you, the observer, collapse those waves into particles. Roughly translated into plain English, you "sense" the waves as particles. You "sense" the energy around you as matter.

As you read this, you are probably sitting on a nice solid seat. It's not empty space, you would argue, as you can feel it and it is supporting your body. True. But it is all in your head. You have created this as your perception of the energy universe you live in. That feeling of the support the chair is giving you? In your head. The thing you see as your chair. In your head. The entire universe is, in fact, inside your head. Bizarre as this may sound, it is the truth.

Are you ready for the red pill?

If you keep going down this rabbit hole, it gets truly weird. At any moment, there are an infinite number of potential worlds, and it is you, the observer, who determines which is the one you observe. Don't believe me? Then look up Schrödinger's cat.

Then there is the concept of *"spooky action at a distance."* That sounds like something I just made up, right? Einstein said it to describe a strange feature of quantum mechanics, and a man called John Stuart Bell came up with the proof in 1964. This particular feature is called *entanglement*, and what it means will blow your mind.

Entanglement is the idea that two particles a universe apart can somehow appear to communicate (spooky action at a distance) in that until observed, the position in space and other properties of the particle are indefinite or can be anything essentially. However, when one of the particles is observed and its speed, location and other properties measured, then the other entangled particle properties become strongly correlated.

For example, to make this understandable, if you observe one particle spinning in one direction, then the other spins in the opposite. This implies an instantaneous connection between particles or waves over infinite distance. Knowing this, do you still believe that mind-to-mind communication is science-fiction or woo-woo? You do? Well, look at this experiment that achieved mind-to-mind communication then[1].

You see, when a certain kind of scientist tells you the paranormal is woo-woo, they are telling you a blatant lie. Not only does the quantum world support paranormal and magical phenomena and give it a basis, but the quantum theories are also not actually new. If you were to study magic —real magic—and esotericism, you would soon discover that all that quantum physics talks about today was already known 2,000+ years ago, albeit talked about with a different lexicon or set of terms and kept secret.

So, let's get back to liminal people or beings.

In some quantum-level theories, there is no need for multiple dimensions. Everything exists in one space but on different frequency levels. We cannot see, hear, or sense these parallel worlds because we are unable to do so. Our 'radio receiver' is tuned to a certain band of frequencies, and that is it. The parallel worlds cannot interact and live oblivious to each other most of the time.

Except what if there were times, moments, moods, and so on when those parallel worlds overlapped? Or rather, when the occupants of them had their perception bandwidths altered? Then, on the liminal edge of their reality, they would sense (see, hear, feel etc.) something unknown to them previously.

Imagine this. You are surrounded by shadows, demons, malevolent beings all the time and are oblivious to it. Well, most of the time. And they are oblivious to you—or are they?

4

LIMINAL BEINGS

In my research into the Black-Eyed Kids, I started to see some interesting patterns in the stories. First, it seemed to me that the *modus operandi* or key characteristics of how the Black-Eyed people interacted with us was different depending upon the social and cultural background of the people having the experience. The typical on-the-doorstep story of young kids screaming, "Let me in!" at 4am and terrorizing people in North America isn't the way that they are known in the UK, for example.

In the UK, Black-Eyed Kids are ghosts and seen in forests and other out-of-the-way places. Same beings but very different story lines. Except that when you have an American living in London, they still appear to that person as young kids on the doorstep. In other words, the way the BEK manifest appears to have some cultural and social aspect to it. Another example is the Black-Eyed adult who sits in Wal-Mart parking lots asking people by their first name for something—this type of experience only seems to happen in North America.

Next, despite the person recounting their experience of the kids as noisy—banging for hours on the door screaming let me in and so on—apparently, no one else heard them at all. Yet, the kids did often leave evidence of having been there.

In one story I related in my BEK book, one child was eating an apple. The apple was found half-eaten on the doorstep, even though none of the neighbors heard anything. In another story, the kids' footprints were visible in the snow, yet again, despite the harrowing experience had by the occupant of the house, no one around heard a thing. There are many other examples of this showing that the BEK had been there, yet no one else saw or heard them at all.

There are other weird things about the BEK stories I collected as well. One would be the stories on high-security armed-forces bases. How on earth do small, unusually dressed kids get on an air-force base in the dead of night?

There is one harrowing story I am fond of telling in interviews about a couple travelling to Texas, who encounter a gas station and a small BEK-like child who insists on being taken fishing. This one seems to take place outside of time as the gas station appears to be from another era, filled with old

Coke bottles and other stock and is not known to the sympathetic waitress who listens to the story told by the distraught couple, not a mile or two farther along the road. In that encounter, it isn't just the kid who seems not to exist beyond the experience of the couple but the entire gas station as well.

I have also had hundreds of stories related to me regarding shadow people, and these shadow people really do seem to be as surprised at our existence as we are by theirs. In many stories, the shadow becomes aware of the observer and runs away from them as if scared, too.

Here is one example.

I have lived in the same house since 1996, and it was built in 1987. Fast forward to 2006. Myself, my husband, and our two kids lived a regular family life. No strange activity in our house until the eventful day. It was evening, and I was with my daughter in the kitchen, we turned off the lights and made our way to the staircase to go upstairs. I turn the corner, and there was a solid black figure standing at the bottom of the stairs. I let out a scream, and my daughter asked, "What's wrong mommy?" I replied, "Nothing, I just scared myself in the dark," because I didn't want to freak her out.

A month went by, and my son came home from University. He turned to me and said, "What the hell is wrong with this house? First, I see a full black figure on the staircase and then half the figure, only from the waist up." We were freaked out because we didn't understand what was going on. I went out and bought sage, we saged the house, said prayers, and we're not even religious people.

A couple of years went by, and we hadn't seen the black figure even though we were having strange things happening like pictures falling off walls, crystal bowl falling off the shelf, doors slamming on their own, and me having sleep paralysis where I was lying on my stomach and my face was pushed into the pillow. A couple of years later, when my daughter was around 13 years old, she came into my room and told me that she wasn't going to sleep in her room because there was something in there. I told her not to be ridiculous, and to prove that there was nothing in her room, I would sleep with her that night.

I was lying facing my daughter, and she was between me and the wall. In the middle of the night I woke up with the feeling that someone was leaning on my arm. All of a sudden a male raspy deep voice whispered in my ear, "Can you hear me?" I was so freaked out that I didn't dare turn around to look. I just started telling whatever it was telepathically that it was not welcome in my home and needed to leave, I also started saying the Lord's Prayer. The next morning my daughter said "See! I was right! I woke up in the middle of the night, and there was a black figure standing right beside you!" I told her it was probably her imagination because I didn't want to scare her. It took about a year before I told her my experience because I wanted her to feel validated.

We went on a vacation and asked my sister and brother-in-law to come and house sit. When we got back from vacation there was a snow globe on my fireplace mantle with the words "Bless

This House." I started laughing and asked my sister-in-law why she had purchased it. Her reply was that my brother-in-law had seen a black figure in our bedroom, and she had heard a child call "Mommy." They were convinced that the house was haunted.

My son grew up, got married, and he and his wife stayed with us for a couple of months until their house closed. She's a nurse and very level headed. She told me, "I woke up in the middle of the night and there was a black mist floating over the bed and then fingers tapping on the nightstand." She said she refused to stay alone in the finished basement, so if my son was away on business she would go to her parents' place.

In 2019, my daughter was home, and I was in my room reading a book, and my husband was also reading. All of a sudden, I saw a black mist come up through the floor and then back down into the floor. I rubbed my eyes thinking maybe my eyes were playing tricks on me. All of a sudden my daughter comes into the room and says "You're not going to believe what I just saw!?" I smiled because I had a feeling I knew what she was going to say. She proceeds to tell us that she had just walked into the bathroom and the black figure was just standing there.

It's obvious that he's still here and every so often makes himself known. We don't know who he is. He's allowed to stay, as long as he doesn't whisper in my ear at night or scare us half to death. Unfortunately, we have never taken a picture of him.

Submitted by Lena Doyle

Here is another one of the many shadow-person encounters in my collection.

The first took place at work, I was a shipper for a small company; my work area was in the basement of an old building. The building was one of those old three-storey industrial brick buildings that you'd have to walk upstairs to get to the first floor. The basement was only 3 feet below ground level, and that is where I spent 8 hours of my day, Monday to Friday. It was a decently lit basement with the florescent lights mounted to the ceiling but not aligned over the aisles very well; there were shelves that ran perpendicular to the white, painted brick, outside walls where we stored finished goods ready to be shipped. I would receive paperwork for orders, fill and prep for shipping, fill out all UPS paperwork, and then wait for the UPS guy. One day I was filling an order, and I was in one of these poorly-lit aisles, there was a little basement window in the outside wall, but it was behind the shelving rack I was picking from, and the ceiling light was in the main aisle but not shining very well into the one I was working in. Then, it happened. As I reached to grab a part box a shadow came across the wall. I looked around, but I was alone in the basement. Mind you this isn't a very large basement, and although we had a receiver who worked down there with me, he was out of the building at the time.

I looked back at my hand, which was still reaching of the part box, and still there against the wall was the shadow. It was then I realized it wasn't a normal shadow, it was dark. Darker than dark, it was the opposite of light, ANY light. I have been in the back of caves in West Virginia with a youth group, and we would turn off our flashlights to experience the complete and utter darkness; and this shadow was that same darkness—if not darker. It moved across the wall and onto the shelving. It moved fluidly and molded itself to any surface it came in contact with, like water moving over a rock. It enveloped all it came in contact with, and as it did, you couldn't define the surface it was on.

Dropping the box, I jumped back and moved quickly into the main aisle. Again, I looked for someone in the basement with me, but there was no one. I was all alone with whatever that shadow was. From the main aisle I could still see it, moving across the wall and shelving, it moved toward the area of the wall that was closer to the window, and as it did, the light on the wall disappeared. Immediately I started praying to Christ to protect me and in His name commanded it to leave. And just as quickly as it appeared it was gone! Light that came through the window onto the wall returned (mind you no light was blocked from coming in the window from the outside, it was still daylight outside, just wherever that thing touched the light was gone on that surface). I went upstairs to use the phone, this was still pre-cell-phone days, and called my mom and asked her to pray with me before I went back down into that basement. I returned to my desk and saw nothing more of the shadow.

I worked in that basement for months and never saw anything like that again, there or anywhere else. I know what I saw, and I'll never forget it. Something that absorbed light, something that obviously feared the name of God was down there that day, something.

Submitted by Shawn Loch

Here is another in which the person reports seeing and hearing shadow people.

Okay, so I know that there is a shadow man, but has anyone experienced shadow people?

This probably sounds super weird, and I think it all started around my 13th birthday. I just got out of a really bad friend group and noticed these strange "beings." I call them "the Beings" because I can't tell if they're man or monster.

Well, it was maybe a week after my 13, and I'd see a shadow that's not mine when I'm in a room by myself. This was two years ago. Skip ahead two years, and everything's sooo much worse! I constantly feel as if I'm watched, and I'm on edge. So much so that any loud, sudden noise, and I'm a complete wreck. I don't know if women are more prone to Beings, but if so, that would have [been] nice to know. My parents won't or can't talk about the dead not resting, but from what I've heard about my parents, they think it's shenannigans. Until recently I thought so too. And now coming up on my 15th, I practically throw up when something scares me! I'm on edge, nervous, and now all of my coworkers call me "Scaredy." Maybe I'm just crazy, but every second of every day feels like I'm being watched, and my heart rate jumps at every sound.

Can I do something about this? I've been told by some "psychics" I have people still "stuck" on me. But they're probably just in it for the money. Has anyone else experienced this too?

Submitted by Devil's Daughter to Weird Darkness and My Haunted Life Too

This story is from Reddit, and I do know that some

people find Reddit stories suspect. I picked it though for a specific reason, so please do bear with me.

Let me be the first to say this is going to be a long post. I wrote it as a means to, I suppose, cope with all that was happening at the time, and while it is the highlights of the insanity that happened, I think that I was genuinely being hunted or... haunted by something evil. Even worse, I wasn't alone in witnessing this thing's work. Let me know what you think.

I was twenty-one years old when my grandmother, who raised me, died of cancer. Her death was an extremely emotional and mental toll that forced me away from college and made me return home to the house she and my grandfather built. It wasn't ever finished, a three-bedroom two-bath home surrounded by the red clay of the country, towering old cedar trees, and surrounded by country folk who were hard-working, God-fearing people. No one could have understood what would happen with her death though. The house no longer felt like a home when I entered the door, dragging my luggage from the dorms inside and to her large walk-in closet. The house belonged to me now, but in truth, I didn't want it.

It was as though she'd never been there. Her clothes were present, as were her jewelry items and the white bedding she loved. But, her laughter no longer resounded with her voice; the warmth she exuded had gone as well, leaving the master bedroom cold and the air stagnant. It was as though the living color and safety that this home once held had been snuffed out with her passing.

Standing there inside this large closet, I suddenly felt anxious, and I gravitated to her clothes that hung neatly in the closet, pulling out a favorite pink shirt and bringing it to my nose to smell it. I wanted to feel like a piece of her was still with me; I wanted to have her scent there one more time, but when I pulled the shirt to do this, there was no scent. It too had been erased it seemed. And that left me feeling all the more empty.

For the first time since the night she died, I found myself crying, standing in this closet with no idea of what to do now that she was gone. My biological mother was living with me at the time, as was my college roommate and my three siblings. Yet, I honestly had never felt more alone. So, I stood there, contemplating what to do next as I tried to cope with losing someone so precious to me and grappling with the reality that the cancer that took her is genetic, and I or someone else could fall victim to it next.

To be honest, putting words to how I felt—and still feel—about all the things that happened during this time is too painful. But it was in her passing that the worst things happened. I had gotten a better grasp on my emotions after a few minutes and wiped my eyes, preparing to leave the closet and shut the door behind me. And then, out of the corner of my eyes, I saw a tall shadowy figure standing in the corner of the room. It had features I could make out but just barely. A tall, thin frame with clawed hands looked like it and was black as night. It exuded this feeling of fear, of misery—the sensation of death.

I walked out of the room and shut the door, never once looking up from the ground before I went to my bedroom where my roommate and sister were. Only when they asked did I realize how pale I was, but I brushed it off with the way things had been—I was tired, heartbroken, and trying to ignore my own grieving process to be strong for my younger siblings. Something that I would regret in later years. But I didn't mention the shadowy figure, hoping it was nothing more than my exhausted brain coming up with whatever it could to make sense of everything that had happened over the last two years between college, my grandfather dying, and now my grandmother. I chalked it up to the stress, to the grief, and to the overwhelming sensations that I couldn't name. That was the worst mistake I could have made.

In the coming months, things began to change. I noticed the shadow in the room whenever the door was open, so I rarely let it stay that way. Yet, sometimes, the kids would leave it open, and I would be face to face with the shadow. Eventually, my mom and youngest brother came to where they were sleeping in that room, my roommate and sister sharing a room with me, and my brother in the third and smallest bedroom. Yet no matter how much I tried to ignore it, something never felt right in the house. It was little things at first, like missing items or small arguments that had happened occasionally. However, that steadily changed into what I can only describe as something malevolent.

More arguments started breaking out, escalating to the point where they bordered on abuse. My siblings were telling me how they didn't feel comfortable in the house like someone was always watching them. My roommate didn't like going into my grandmother's room, and my mom started getting sick. One night, my little brother was going to bed, and it was my job to make sure he went to sleep since my mom was working the night shift at her job. I put him down and was going to turn on the closet light and shut the door behind us when he sat up in bed and told me not to shut the door. He was around six or so at the time, so I didn't think much of it. I was an adult and am still scared of the dark even today, so I imagined he was, too. But then, he told me something that made my blood run cold.

"The shadow man will come close if you shut the door."

And then, I knew he was seeing it, too. I had said nothing, deciding not to give it attention just on the off chance that it wasn't a hallucination. Although, the other two entities that my entire family had seen in the past—a blue dog and a short goblin-like creature with green skin and black veins bearing razor blades for teeth and sharp, thick yellow claws—did come to mind when I first saw it.

But my little brother was scared, and I knew that telling him I could see it, too, would make matters worse. Therefore, I got into the bed with him and told him to not worry about it, that it was a bad dream. I did what any adult would do with a child saying they saw a monster—I pretended it wasn't real if only to give him some comfort. Even while I was staring it down.

After that, though, it only got worse. As the months went on, the entity started moving, drawing closer to the doorway of the bedroom, and each time it did that, there were more arguments and fights taking place. It gave me this indescribable feeling of dread. As though something bad was going to happen if we didn't get rid of it. However, what ended up happening was fixable, if not terrible.

Our home was going into foreclosure, and at twenty-two years old, I was having to cope with losing the house, but at the same time, wanted nothing more to do with it. Selling the home would have been a benefit, but no one was going to buy it no matter what we did. Each potential buyer fell through, time and time again, the arguments were worsening, the monetary circumstances were atrocious, and then one night, my mom took my youngest brother to the grocery store with her, leaving us alone for a few hours while my roommate and I tended to the kids. Something had happened to where my sister and brother got into an argument, and the next thing I knew, I hear a baseball bat collide with a door frame.

It was a distinct sound, a heavy, deafening thud that made a chill go up my spine. I was in the kitchen, where I had a clear view of my grandmother's room, where the shadow now stood by the foot of her bed. My sister started screaming and crying, and I panicked. I ran to get between them, and my brother swung the bat at my head. His eyes were wide, almost wild-looking, and his face was twisted in anger. I told my roommate to grab my sister, and I did the only thing I could think of—told her to take them into my grandmother's closet and lock the door. I pushed my brother back, and we all ran into it, the baseball bat was swung a few more times, but thankfully missed all of us.

We locked the door behind us and sat there in the closet on the ground, huddled together, unsure of what had happened. My sister was safe, my roommate was fine, and so was I—but it terrified me to think of what was happening. I called my mom, and she came back and talked my brother down, deciding after the ordeal of the night was over that it was time to get my brother into therapy. But it kept getting worse.

The house was always cold, we started packing up things to move somewhere because we ultimately lost the house, and my mom and I started getting into terrible arguments that were mostly screaming and shouting. She called me things that I knew she wouldn't, I threw things, hit at walls, and started wanting to commit suicide. And the shadow kept getting closer to the door. Eventually, everything came to a head, and I went across the street to my great-grandmother's with my roommate, my uncle helped us move what I wanted to keep out of the house, and we stayed at my great-grandmother's for almost a year.

During that time, my mom continued to live in the house for a while, often still saying and doing things that weren't normal for her. I didn't speak with my siblings or mother for nearly a year, but things started getting better while I lived with my great-grandmother. I got a job, as did my roommate, we started saving up money to move into an apartment, and my mom finally left the house. We still didn't talk, and my siblings thought I betrayed them, but things were looking up. And then, I saw a creature in the hallway at my grandmother's, and so did my roommate. My great-grandmother started telling us that she was seeing things around the house, and I got the worst feeling that it was the shadow from across the street.

My roommate and I talked about it often, sleeping in the guest bedroom of my great-grandmother's house, sitting up in the middle of the night because we heard strange sounds from the hallway that connected into the living room. It made me feel like something bad was going to happen again, and it did. I lost the job I had because of a knee injury I sustained a few years prior. I had dislo-

cated my right knee out of the socket and put it back in by myself, and despite doing it right, because of the way it had been, there were lasting damages. I had to take a break on a six-hour shift and leaned against the stairwell—this was a two-storey restaurant—to take pressure off my leg because it had seized up, and I couldn't bend my knee. They fired me.

It was frustrating, kind of scary even, because it was beginning to feel like I was cursed. And then, a light shined through with me being able to sell some property I owned, which got my roommate and [me] our first apartment. It was a place in the middle of a not-great area in our state, not far from where I'd grown up. The apartment complex was built like townhomes and was income-based. It was cheap and not great. We slept on a blow-up mattress in our living room for the first four months, eventually getting a bed from my great-grandmother that I still use today.

So, my roommate and I shared a room with one another and my pet chihuahua who sadly passed away in this apartment. Things were okay, not great but okay. I thought that finally, I had put enough space between myself and that thing—but I hadn't, and it was foolish for me to think that. My dog passing had nothing to do with this thing, he'd accidentally gotten into some chemicals and passed from those—blame pest control for spraying and not even telling me they had come by—and my roommate still had her job, but I no longer did, so I was often alone in this apartment.

I went downstairs, planning on fixing something to eat and going back upstairs to do some writing and do a bit of work that *my therapist had suggested I do. Things were fine, though I was coping with the loss of my dog, whom I viewed as a child—I had bottle-fed him and everything—and it hurt. But, I was doing alright, and then I saw it again. It was standing in the corner of the living room, but this time, I could see better. I made eye contact with this entity. And it smiled.*

The sight of it made me sick to my stomach. And I fled the kitchen and up the stairs, locking the door to my room behind me. I had a panic attack, and things just spiraled from there. My relationship with my mom was improving, but I was getting worse, having mood swings, panic attacks, anger spells, and outright becoming more and more aggressive atop having trouble with asthma and body pains. During my time at this apartment, I ended up being diagnosed with fibromyalgia and bipolar disorder.

Finally, I suspected that the entity was now just a thing that was because of my mental illness, and started medication for it. I was doing okay, I had gotten another dog—whom I still own, she's three as of writing this story—and I was making progress on coming to terms with everything that had happened. Yet, there's always more to the story, isn't there?

My roommate began seeing the entity, too, and it was edging closer to the stairwell, eventually coming to stand by the front door and then the stairs. We would run upstairs at night after shutting the lights off, leaving the landing light at the top of the stairs on, and sleep with the tv going at night. It was scary and confusing. Why was it following me? What did it want? I began to question these things, and each night, it drew closer and closer to the bedroom. And then, one day—it finally came inside the room.

I had never had sleep paralysis before, but I had always imagined it was scary. And I was right, it is. The first one I had was on a bright summer day. My roommate was playing a video game, and I was sleeping in because I hadn't gotten much sleep the night before—things were fine until I had a sleep paralysis episode. I woke up from my nap, and my whole body was frozen. I couldn't move, I couldn't blink, and breathing was difficult. I knew I was awake because I could hear my roommate playing the game, my dog was sleeping on the bed next to me, and things were normal. Except for the entity that now had a face.

For the first time in a year since I had begun seeing this thing, I saw what it truly looked like. Tall, emaciated, blackened flesh like it had been burned, long sharp nails of equal color, fanged teeth, and white eyes that bore no pupil or iris. Atop its head were antler-like horns, and it crouched to fit into the corner of the room. I stared at it, in fear, in panic and doubt, and thinking that it was going to kill me. It smiled, exposing an evil grin that split up to its ears in a garish Glasgow grin. I wanted to believe I was having a nightmare, that this creature was just a figment of my imagination, and then it walked over to me and grabbed me by the throat. I felt corpse-like cold fingers touch my skin and putrid breath that stunk of decay on my face, and it spoke to me.

"You will never escape me."

And I sat up screaming. I went into a panic attack, my mental state went downhill, and I considered committing suicide again. It hurt me consistently, and the entity didn't leave. I would wake up with bruises, strange scrapes that shouldn't have been there, and even a bite once. It was hard to even come to terms with these things happening. I felt like I was being hunted.

My roommate saw it on several occasions, and so did other people. Stating that the apartment was freezing constantly, that it reeked of something rotting, and mold began to grow on the walls, in the hinges of the doors and vents. It was everywhere, and my roommate and I just left. We moved out nine months after living there, and she got a better job. Our second apartment was great. It was in the city, thirty minutes away from the thing that had haunted us. We were doing good, had a nice home, good finances finally, and things were looking up.

Eventually, though, my mom had to come to stay with us due to her having to move apartments. Her old one had bugs and other unsavory things, but worst of all was the story that my sister told me about a woman in a bloodied dress with matted hair that stood in her stairwell at night—and whispered about how she liked to kill families. It terrified me. I was beginning to think there was no end in sight with these things. I told her not to worry about it, that God would protect us, and that she just needed to pray, and it would help—because it had for me. I started praying a lot, and while I'm not what I would deem an ideal Christian, I do pray for safety and try to do what's right.

But these things wouldn't go away. A year after we moved into the second apartment, we were moving out. Rats, black widow spiders, mold, peeling floors, and rotting walls, you name it—it happened. We both started getting sick, and we both saw the thing again, standing by the fireplace. My heart sank when that happened. Eventually, my mom and siblings moved into a current townhome that they are renting, and my roommate and I moved into an apartment even farther away from my hometown, but still in the same state. We now live almost an hour away from where I grew up, and while that particular entity hasn't shown up save for one time—other things have happened.

My sleep paralysis went through the roof, nightmares about drowning or burning alive—things I fear the most—the entity stalking me, and a corpse sitting at the foot of my bed talking about things that were too rushed and whispered for me to make out. Though, something told me I didn't want to know what it said. And then, there's the good ghost. A nurse walks around at night, peering into our rooms to check on us. She's warm and kind and feels like something safe and compassionate. A stark contrast to whatever has been hunting us.

We now have two dogs and a cat, our apartment is small, and we're seeking a house within the next year. But, during the pandemic, in 2020, my sister told me about a ghost who's in a trash bag and sits up in the kitchen at their place. She came over, and it was there in the middle of the night. A visible shadow appeared on our walls two weeks later, and my roommate and I swore things were trying to come out of it. But, the nurse spirit? She spoke and said it wasn't allowed here. We both heard it, we still hear her walking around at night, along with a white cat spirit that plays with my cat sometimes.

The trash-bag ghost was seen by my mom and other siblings but seems to have left them alone now. I still think about all of this, and it scares me to consider what might happen if it comes back. Thanks to my friends who come from different religions and *backgrounds coming together to pray for our safety, and one of my Wiccan friends sent me a bag of protection herbs. I have Bibles in the house tucked away safely for needs, and I keep salt by my window sills—a thing my mom told me to do—and dream catchers [in] both bedrooms.*

You can believe, call me crazy, say I'm bringing it on myself for whatever reason you so desire. But the reality of it is, these things are real, ghosts, angels, demons, the supernatural does exist. And as my grandmother once said:

"Once you are aware of it, it will always be aware of you."

In truth, you cannot fight these things alone. If you do, believe me, I only caution you to remember that the paranormal can be dangerous, it can be wonderful or horrible. But, you don't have to believe me. I just thought I should warn you.

Originally submitted by Mikunitsune94 on Reddit

The two bits of this story that got my attention were the link with sleep paralysis and the idea that once you are aware of it, it will be aware of you. It echoes something I hear a lot with the BEK, and that is once you know about them, you will experience them. Here is another encounter from Thomas Bauerle, author of a wonderful book on Japanese ghosts[1].

My family moved into a new house in Nagoya, Japan. The first week was all chaos, as we were still unpacking boxes, rearranging furniture, etc. On the first floor, there was a long hallway that led from the front door to the kitchen. One afternoon, as I was walking down the hallway, I felt a sudden urge to turn and look behind me. I was startled to see a tall man in the shape of a featureless black shadow moving down the hallway close behind me.

As he moved along the hallway, he seemed to radiate a small aura of darkness around him, casting a shadow in all directions, blotting out the light on the floor, the walls and the ceiling in a murky circle around him as he moved along the passageway. I stepped into a doorway and watched him hurry past me until he disappeared out of sight at the other end of the hallway.

I really didn't know what to think about what I had seen, but it wasn't the first time I had encountered a ghostly presence, and I didn't get any really bad feeling from the Shadow Man, so I chose to ignore it. Maybe I was just too tired from moving, and I was seeing things that weren't there.

The next day, I was resting on the sofa on the second floor with my wife after a hard day of unpacking. Out of the blue, she turned to me and said, "Have you seen the Shadow Man?" Then she told me she had seen him walking along the hallway downstairs. I told her that I had seen the same guy in the same place earlier that same day. After discussing it a while, we both decided that neither of us had sensed anything malignant about the Shadow Man, so we just decided to let things be.

Two days later, I was climbing up the stairs to the second floor when I met the Shadow Man coming down the stairs toward me. This time he seemed very aware of my presence, as he halted and stood still in front of me. Even though I couldn't make out any features on his face, I could feel a sense of shock and fear coming from him. He turned and fled up the stairs, moving away from me as fast as he could. We have been in the house for 3 years since then, and no one has encountered the Shadow Man again. I'm not sure what it was about me that frightened the Shadow Man, but evidently it was enough to drive him from our house.

This experience is telling us that plainly, whatever shadow man was, he was just as scared of Thomas as Thomas was of him. But this isn't the only example of that kind of interaction; I also found this on a discussion board.

Have I got a story for you!

I was dog sitting for a friend in Queens one evening. I had the TV on, popcorn in hand, and the dog, a muscly (but very sweet) pitbull snoozing next to me. The front door was in view in this very small apartment on the third floor, and all doors and windows were locked. Suddenly, the pup perked up and deeply growled. She jumped up and ran around the corner into the kitchen. I follow her. Standing in the middle of the kitchen is a shadow person. I could barely see the counter behind it, and it looked vaguely whispy around the edges. Roughly six feet tall. Just standing there, looking at the dog. The dog stops, hackles raised, growling at the thing and barking. I gasp, the thing turns to look at me and takes a step back, almost in shock (maybe it was shocked that I could see it?) I quickly yell at it to leave, tell it that it is NOT welcome here, and that it can NEVER come back. It walks through a wall. The dog and I eventually calm down... but that was one of the best paranormal experiences I've had.

Originally a comment by Tatiana Philip-Therese Federoff on Buzzfeed

The shadow people often seem oblivious to our presence, and in one or two instances, they are surprised seeing us possibly as the paranormal entity that intrudes into their reality and scares them. However, the next encounter goes a step farther and shows how a shadow person not only became aware of the person seeing it but began to interact in a disturbing manner.

A friend of mine suggested I send this story into your site. I have read many of your stories—but I've seen nothing like this. I thought your readers might be interested in my story.

I moved to Connecticut with my family around the time that I had started first grade. Soon after I began seeing dark figures in my room at night. You couldn't really make out any features other than that they had tall, broad shoulders and wide chests which made me think they were adult men. None of them had faces. They would pay no attention to me and walk around the room without interfering in anything I was doing. These events didn't happen every night, and the nights that they did happen I sometimes would have some very scary nightmares.

At first this was very frightening, but after I had seen that they would not hurt me I grew used to them being there. One night was different, though. We had been living in the house for a little over three or four years, one night I had just climbed into bed and said goodnight to the figures which had become part of my routine.

For the first time one of them responded and said good night back to me. I was very startled from this, but I continued to talk to him. I don't remember the entire conversation, but what I do remember is that he introduced himself and told me that he wasn't there to hurt me. This spirit and I became good friends, and I began to see him during the day.

After a couple of years, he and I became so close that I allowed him to actually climb into my body. He had a term for this that I can't remember. After this happened I stopped seeing the dark figures in my room. I and this spirit would still talk; I would "think" things, and he would "think" them back to me. It became an addiction for me to spend time with him.

It wasn't until I was about seventeen years old that he began to use my body without my permission; because of this I got very upset with him and told him to leave my body. And I never saw him again. He just disappeared along with the other figures I used to see.

Submitted by Sammi Teal

Another entity to consider is the one seen and experienced during sleep paralysis known as the Old Hag. I dedicated an entire book[2] to this phenomenon and came to a surprising conclusion. That was that sleep paralysis doesn't create the Old Hag effect but that the Old Hag entity uses sleep paralysis to manifest. The Old Hag and similar entities like the woman with the long hair parted in the middle and so on are also joined by shadow people in many experiences of sleep paralysis. Sometimes, the Old Hag gets sexual as well, and the experience becomes erotic. A novelist called Robert Moss has also described the experience of being visited by a horrific hag which transforms into a beautiful woman. Moss remembers how, as a teenager, a horrible hag-like creature with many arms and floppy, withered breasts entered his room and attacked him. He lay paralyzed as the entity moved up the bed, stood on his chest, and then lowered herself onto him. Moss explains how.

Despite my disgust, I am aroused, and now she is riding me. Her teeth are like daggers. My chest is spattered by blood and foulness from the rotting heads. There is nothing for me to do but stay with this. I tell myself I will survive. At last, the act is done. Satisfied, the nightmare hag transforms into a beautiful young woman. She smells like jasmine, like sandalwood. She takes me by the hand to a forest shrine. I forget about the body I have left frozen in the bed.

From among the collection of encounter stories, I picked a couple more to illustrate the Old Hag experience.

I had a period in my late 20s when I wasn't necessarily doing that well—drinking too much, which left my nervous system shredded and vulnerable.

I woke up in sleep paralysis while living in my mom's basement, with a spectral hag floating not far above me, maybe six inches. Classic banshee form—skeletal face, half-rotted in parts, cheekbones exposed, gaping mouth, eye sockets, stringy hair.

I just freaked and froze, not that I would've been able to do anything anyway, as I couldn't move.

I was living in a semi-raw, semi-unfinished basement at the time, with styrofoam insulation in the ceiling. I watched, in real-time, as the specter gradually went from 3D to 2D, becoming a shape and a texture of ceiling insulation that completely matched the skeletal hag I had just been seeing. It leaves you wondering if it's your unconscious mind putting pieces together and making patterns or if it was a true visitation.

That house is haunted, and those spirits DID NOT like me. Either way, I don't intend on going back to verify.

Submitted by Forestpunk

I took a nap midday once. Slight lucid dream, nothing spectacular. Woke up to sounds of people talking outside my bay window and moving my porch furniture. I tried to get up to stop them but realized I was in sleep paralysis. Talked myself through it blinking frequently. The sounds go away, but a shadow starts growing in the corner of my living room. Just keep telling myself its sleep paralysis, but the shadow turns into this very tall black shadow of a witch with black tattered robes hanging off her and long claws. She walks up to me and gets her face close to mine and vanishes, and I can move again. It really bothered me. I don't scare easily, but she was the embodiment of things that scare me.

Submitted by FarmPhreshScottdog on Reddit in response to a post by G. Michael Vasey

These types of entities—BEK, shadow people, the Old Hag, and so on—are forms of liminal entities. I suggest that they exist in a different bandwidth that is lower than ours, and sometimes they stray into our frequency, becoming the source of nightmares and horror for those who experience them. I also now believe that demons and other dark entities are also from parallel worlds that live side by side with ours.

In my Old Hag experience, riding on an overnight train in Europe a couple of years ago, what disturbed me more than anything was that this entity was clearly visible to me as a smoky shapeless mass sitting in the luggage rack in between sleep paralysis experiences. I surmised that it was stalking the occupants of that rail cabin. This is what happened in my experience.

I like trains and riding by train so when an opportunity to go to Frankfurt for business presented itself, I opted to take the sleeper service in both directions rather than fly. I was looking forward to the trip, and as I found my private sleeper compartment at Vienna station, I will admit to a little excitement. I had decided to try to get some sleep almost immediately [when] the train left Vienna as arrival was at 5.25am, meaning I would need to wake up about an hour earlier. I pushed the three seats away and pulled down the bed, and after ordering breakfast, I got into bed and switched off the light. For a while, I just lay there allowing myself to be gently rocked to sleep by the motion of the train.

At some point, I recall feeling as if someone was sitting on my legs, and as I tried to get up to see, I realised that I could not. I could not move! I could hear the people next door talking and the sound of the train on the tracks and something getting up off my legs and moving above me. There was a feeling of rising terror especially when I saw the thing that now floated above me. It was like a whitish mist with eyes and a face of sorts. It came alongside me and peered at me. I tried to scream for help. Nothing came out. I was totally aware of everything—sounds, smells, sight, my fear —everything—but I was paralyzed and the plaything of whatever this was that was now inspecting me like a cold piece of meat.

Then, as quickly as it had started, the train suddenly braked, and the jolt freed me. I watched as the mist rose up and into the luggage recess of the carriage where it seemed to be waiting. I sat up and switched on the light. It was still there. I was frightened, and my heart was racing. I was also puzzled. What had just happened? Had it been a vivid dream? I soon came to the conclusion it was an Old Hag experience or sleep paralysis, and that hadn't happened to me in decades. Despite that, the thing—the entity—was real. I could still see it.

When you write ghost stories for a hobby, it takes something very scary to frighten you. I can tell you that I felt a mixture of fear and puzzlement. I started to pray and then also do some self protection. The thing seemed to have gone, and I commanded it not to bother me again. After a few minutes, I lay down again and dozed.

I awoke knowing the thing was back. Once again, I could not move nor scream, yet I could see, hear, and sense everything. The thing was hovering over me, and I'll be honest here, I felt a sense of sexual excitement along with the fear. The thing was going to molest me? For a few moments, it seemed so, but then it seemed to know that I was aware of it and its intentions, and instead, it moved upwards and peered at me again.

I started to scream, 'Help, help me,' but no sound emerged from my lips. I was now really scared because I was at the mercy of this thing, and we both knew it, and there was not a thing I could do. Imagine lying paralyzed as an entity—perhaps even a succubus —eyed you up as its next victim. I continued to struggle, though I could not move. I kept on trying to scream for help. I knew there was a call button just above my head if only I could move. The malevolence of the thing was scaring me and I knew it was just a matter of time before it started doing whatever it planned on doing...

And then, again, I was fully awake and able to move. I sat up sweating profusely with my heart pounding. I again prayed, engaged in some self protection, and generally told it to get the hell away from me. Needless to say, I barely rested the remainder of the night, and my day was one of a heavy tiredness dogged by the memory of the grayish mist-like face.

The Old Hag experience certainly has a sexual aspect to it, and it naturally leads us to the phenomenon of ghost lovers as liminal entities. I covered this at length in my book on the topic, but suffice to say, these are entities that seem to use lust and sex as a way to gain energy from their victims. However, here is one shocking account of such a being in a long-term relationship, and again, notice how that relationship turns as the human involved starts to lose interest.

(What's a girl to do when her elusive lover won't return her calls?)

My story's not new. I'm not the first woman to fall in love only to be deserted.

Shocking he would do something so shady, because up to that point he had been so transparent.

It started out passionately. Out of thin air he arrived, and our first time together was amazing! For 2-3 hours he ravished me, over and over and over....

Words not coming easily to him, he used songs to assure me of his love and how perfect he thought I was. I was smitten, always giving in when I felt his presence.

For months we had clandestine meetings, but he had a tendency to disappear. I worried he was married, since he always came to me, not me to him. And over time the sex became more and more lackluster. I tried having meaningful conversations with him, but they were all one-sided.

Still, for months in the summer of 2014, when I was ill, he was there for me. He reminded me of Gregory Peck in To Kill a Mockingbird...the strong silent type.

At the age of 52, after decades of fruitless searching, I had finally found "the one."

But eventually I saw right through him. I noticed that, despite his obvious physical attraction to me and assurances of love and marriage, aside from smoky "vapors," nothing ever manifested. My mysterious, enigmatic lover would only visit me when I was alone, my friends and family never meeting him.

Was he ashamed of me?

Something seemed fishy. I started to suspect he was full of sh-t, so much I could smell it on him. Sh-t and death. He reeked of it. But eventually the odors, along with the ardor, faded.

His intentions were clear; I could see right through him. I was a boo-ty call.

He must have preferred me submissive, because as I became well his visits came farther and farther apart. He no longer put any effort into the lovemaking, and I became dissatisfied, never admitting it to him, hoping somehow things could go back to the way they were in the beginning.

Things swiftly turned from heaven to h-ll. As I felt the pin pricks and pinches, I began to awake covered in bruises and scratches from his visits. Funny, I didn't remember his hurting me, although I suspected he drugged me as I developed temporary amnesia.

In spite of everything, after he was gone, I begged him to come back. But he refused to speak to me.

After our last meeting, I thought of how we had met. I was vulnerable at the time, ill with an airborne fungal infection that can go to the central nervous system causing delusions and hallucinations. The infection gave me seizures, migraines, insomnia, wild mood swings, symptoms of multiple sclerosis, and temporary blindness.

My lover gone, I fell into a deep depression, barely able to bathe or brush my teeth. Incredibly disappointed, more than a little confused, and feeling utterly alone, I spent 50-80% of most days sobbing uncontrollably and contemplating suicide.

But eventually I'd find my way out of the darkness. And the depression, like my lover, vanished into thin air.

Only later would I realize that I had been having a passionate affair with a fungus, and yet it STILL wasn't the dumbest thing I had ever dated.

Submitted by Susan MacIntyre

Just as importantly, note her comments about how she felt when they first met—an airborne fungal infection creating delusions and hallucinations.

In the case of the BEK, the Old Hag, and demonic beings, it seems that they are aware of us. They know of our existence. In fact, it seems that we have something they want and need, and that thing seems to be energy. The energy takes the form of fear, lust, jealousy, and so on, and they engage in activities designed to elicit those emotions from us and then to feed upon our emotional energies. They are like vampires of energy. Perhaps the energy they can steal from us raises their vibrational state a little.

Shadow people seem a little different in that they seem to be liminal people that live in the reality next to ours, and quite often, that liminal boundary between our realities dissolves a little where they become our shadow men or boogiemen, and we perhaps become theirs.

It isn't all bad, though. At the other end of the bandwidth scale, we can encounter beings of a higher vibration from time to time. I have fewer of these sorts of encounter stories in my collection, but they usually go something like these.

Christmas morning, 1993. I was twelve years old. I had woken early, before anyone else in the house and was lying in bed trying to get up the nerve to go downstairs to my presents. A bright light shone under my door and then started coming into the room. Soon the room was completely filled with this bright light, and I could barely make out a figure standing in my room. The next thing I remember is waking up a few hours later. I have no idea what this was, but my mom said it must have been a visitation from an angel. I wish I were able to recall more details. Has anyone else experienced anything like this? The light was so bright, warm, and welcoming.

Submitted by James R.

I have been a medium since I can remember, and my first encounter was when I was about 6 years old. I had a nightmare, so I was going to go into my parents' room. When I reached the hallway, I saw a woman with long dark hair and a flowing white dress. She was staring into my parents' bedroom. I couldn't believe what I was seeing. I rubbed my eyes, and when I looked at her again she turned [and] smiled at me, the way a loving mother would smile at a child. I didn't know what to do, I charged down the hall waving my hands in front of me, and just before I would have touched her she vanished. I woke up my mom, who told me it was a dream and to go to sleep.

The next morning, knowing full well that it wasn't a dream as my mom had said, I went to investigate the spot where the woman was standing. In that spot I found a single, small white feather.

When I was little, and being a medium, I thought she was a ghost. Now I believe that I saw a guardian angel, as it was a few weeks later that my parents got into a car accident on the interstate where they were hit head on. She knew I needed my parents, and it wasn't their time to go, she was protecting them. After finding that feather, I will always be a believer... After all, seeing is believing. (Rachael West, aka Ms. Riggs).

Submitted by Rachael West

When I was a child I would regularly awake to see an "angel" standing at the bottom of my bed. This would happen at least three or four times a month. This angel gave off such a white glow that I would often have to shield my eyes. I could see it was a female figure because her hair was long and golden. I could never make out any features on her face. She would just stand at the bottom of my bed and look down at me. I never felt threatened or *scared and actually missed her when she stopped visiting me physically.*

I have often been lucky in my life, and I do believe she is my spirit guide. A few things happened that I feel she made happen. One of those instances was a sudden urge to go and see my mom, which took me away from my home. I had this overpowering need to see mom, and when I arrived we had dinner together. After dinner she switched on the TV news. The news was reporting an automobile crash that I would have been in the middle of had I gone directly home from work. That desire probably saved my life.

I strongly believe in the afterlife and in guardian angels. I wish people would spend more time thinking about the wonderful things that surround us—rather than the negatives of the real world.

Submitted by Alec McDale

All of us are familiar with stories of angelic interventions often called third-man encounters. These are mysterious beings on the edge of reality that appear and help us at times of great need. One well-known story involves that of Charles Lindbergh, who recounted how as he tried not to fall asleep while flying across the Atlantic solo in 1927, his airplane, *The Spirit of St. Louis*, was filled with vague forms who helped him.

Another story involves the events of 9/11, when Ron DiFrancesco heard a voice telling him to get up, and he sensed a physical presence that encouraged him. The same being led him through the flames in the stairwell, and he made his way to safety as one of only 4 people who escaped from above the 81st floor.

There are many, many stories of this sort of encounter, and yet they often get less press than the other darker stories of BEK, shadow beings, and demons. However, I think these are also liminal people or beings who also seem to know of our existence and who can, it seems, enter our reality in times of need.

There are other forms of beings that guide and aid people as well-known as spirit guides. These entities will use their human contact to channel knowledge through and include well-known guides like the Seth, for example. These beings can be aliens, spirits, angels, or guardian angels, and the person experiencing them is said to be channeling. Several channelers have made high-profile livings sharing the "wisdom" received from their contacts selling books, making videos, and holding classes and lectures, including people like Paul Sehlig, Jane Roberts, and many more. Often, what these contacts have to say is very uplifting, spiritual, and enlightening.

I, too, have a contact (more than one in fact) who developed, as I did, a five-year course in magic (real magic—not stage magic) with a school of occult studies in the UK. I have outlined how I met this inner contact in some detail in my first book, *Inner Journeys*[3].

An example of this was a series of meditations that I was engaged in shortly after my crucifixion experience. I kept seeing and hearing what appeared to be 'AR' or 'AZ' or something similar.

I dutifully wrote it down. Reading back through my dairy one day, I noticed that these two letters kept coming up over and over again, and so, I began asking what this meant. In answer to my question, I found myself in a tunnel with water running in it. I often see tunnels during meditation, and so, I was not greatly surprised. I had a sword in my hand, and for some reason I decided to hack at the side of the tunnel with it. As I hacked a hole in the tunnel, I could see blue sky and sunlight outside. When the hole was large enough, I stepped through and found myself on the side of a very steep mountain in the most amazing mountainous desert country.

As I looked around this landscape, I noticed a small huddled figure sat on the mountainside dressed from head to foot in grey robes.

"Who are you?" I asked.

"Asteroth," was the reply.

Asteroth is the name I use to describe this inner contact that sometimes "speaks" to me. But what or who is Asteroth? Well, Asteroth appears to me as a woman, and I have often suspected she is my own higher self or an aspect of it, anyway—my anima. At other times, I'm not so sure, and I see her as more of a guardian angel who occasionally tells me things of spiritual value and guides me. The mode of communication is also interesting as it is not a voice and conversation but more of a seed thought that arrives in my mind and unpacks itself there. For that reason, I find it difficult sometimes to express in words what I learn from her.

As an example, Asteroth once gave me the seed thought

—love is acceptance—and then this unpacked itself instantaneously, filling my mind with ideas, concepts, and values all related to that statement. I cover this also in *Inner Journeys*.

Recently, I had another experience of a contact, and this one was rather different. Standing in the archeological remains of a Slavic rotunda church in the middle of a place called Mikulčice in Moravia, I was meditating and particularly trying to meditate on why all Slavic churches seem to have earth-energy lines running down their aisles. Did the Slavs know this?

I became aware of a presence, a man, standing nearby. In my mind's eye, he was a rugged man but not young, with white hair and beard, dressed in off-white loose clothing, holding a thick staff. I asked him who he was and struggled for several minutes to understand his response. Eventually, I understood his name to be Vlk Vzduch or similar, which, in Czech, approximates to Wolf's Breath. He then told me in words that the Slavs saw the earth energies as lines of light and worked with them.

I have talked to others who have personal contacts—inner contacts, guides, or whatever you want to call them—and some hear them speaking words while others have the seed though and unpacking experience. Whatever phenomenon this is, it is widespread and strong, associated with meditation and spiritual enlightenment. Perhaps you also have had this type of experience.

Another type of encounter with the higher worlds is the near-death experience, and accounts of near-death are quite commonplace. The experience in a nutshell usually involves a feeling of peace and acceptance accompanied by a light or a tunnel filled with light and the appearance of a being who is the essence of love itself. The person experiencing near-death is then given a choice or is told their time is not up yet, and they need to return. On returning, their lives are often completely and utterly changed by the experience, and they are convinced of the existence of God and an afterlife. They become more spiritual people. The near-death experience is a game changer.

This example account was sent into my website.

When I was nine years old I was a very ill child due various illnesses. I was constantly in and out of hospitals. At one point I had been sick for a long time, and by all accounts, I was close to death. All I can remember is seeing what looked like a man surrounded by light. No facial features, no distinctive marks—just the figure of a man bathed in life.

He asked me directly if I was ready to go. I didn't want to go and wanted to live. He explained that he would never hurt me, but I kept wondering what would happen to my parents. It was then that I felt completely filled with love and energy. The figure was gone, but that feeling remained with me for a long time afterwards.

With my health in the state it was in, I should have suffered more than I did. I didn't die, and I'm alive today to take care of my parents. Every now and then I still feel the energy of that being taking care of me—healing me from within.

Here is another one to show just how similar this sort of experience is.

I had a few experiences with the paranormal in my life. I've had a few runins with ghosts. Those are stories for another time. Today, I want to share my story of a near-death experience when I was a kid. For a long time I never shared with anyone out of fear of not being believed. I am past that now, and here goes my story.

One summer day, the end of my third grade year, my best friend invited me to come along to go down to the neighborhood creek. We lived in a small town in Wisconsin, and the creek was a wooded area behind a park down the street from our house. My friend Crystal, along with her uncle, step-dad, and me, walked through the small wooded area to the creek. We decided to just get in the water and walk it to see where it would lead us. Not a smart idea for two girls who couldn't swim, but, hey, we trusted the adults.

As we walked, talked, and played, we noticed the water had gotten deeper. The water was waist deep on my friend and me so the guys came up with the idea to put us on their shoulders. Crystal's uncle put me on his shoulders, and Crystal's step-dad had her on his shoulders. As soon as they had us comfortably on shoulders and taken their first step we all went down. There was a dropoff underneath the water!

I panicked! Trying to swim up to the surface for air but couldn't quite get there. Someone from below pushed me up, but yet again, I couldn't reach the surface. All I kept thinking about was my Mom, how she would never find me because I was going to die. How hurt she would be. I prayed and asked God not to let *me die. I kept saying this in my mind. Then at my last breath I thought to myself there is no God.*

Right then I saw a white light, a tunnel. A man's voice spoke and called me by name. I walked this beautiful tunnel of light following the voice. I saw a beautiful, curly-hair little girl dressed in all white smiling at me. As I continued to walk I felt peace, and I didn't want to leave. I don't have any memory of what happened during that time. All I remember hearing [is] the man's voice tell me I have to go back and the words "when I call, come."

No one knows how this happened. On the way home we all were silent until Crystal's uncle asked what happened. Crystal and her dad were on the other side of the creek from where her uncle and I were. The uncle told us when he tried to push me up he notice I wasn't moving. In fact he thought I had drowned because I looked frozen stiff in the water. The men tried saving us. The miracle happened when we all came forth from the water, my friend Crystal was on her step-dad's shoulders, I was on Crystal's uncle's shoulders coming up onto the shore in shallow water. No one could figure out what happened. I never told my story with them that day, and now I wish I had. They very well may have believed me.

Submitted by Veronica Steward to Weird Darkness and My Haunted Life Too

After collecting stories from hundreds if not thousands of people and having a wide range of personal experiences as well, I am forced to conclude that our reality is not what it seems to be. You can, of course, take the materialist-reductionist approach and scoff at all paranormal phenomena as bunkum and woo-woo, but there is an entire body of science that supports their existence and allows us to postulate what might be going on. In fact, to deny outright that these things do not exist is one way to ensure that in your reality, they don't. It is why when there are skeptics around, some phenomena never occur. The skeptic is creating their reality at the quantum level, and this reality doesn't allow for anything like paranormal phenomena. But if we live in a universe that is half as strange as quantum scientists theorize, then there is no real scientific basis for denying any of these strange beings and effects.

This theory also can be applied equally well to other paranormal and mythological beings and phenomena. Fairies might be an immediate example. The Irish Sidhe (pronounced *shee*) come to mind instantly. According to Dr. Kelly Fitzgerald from the School of Irish, Celtic Studies and Folklore at University College Dublin, "*When one begins to explore the role of the supernatural in traditional Irish society, it really is a parallel world in coexistence with this world. They [Sidhe] are not small, tiny figures but [instead] look like the human race. But everything is better in their world—the food tastes better, the music is sweeter, and so on. They do need to draw on the human world occasionally, like when one of their women is about to give birth—they need a midwife—or if they are a player down for a hurling match and so on.*"

The Sidhe are said to have evolved from a mythological people known as the Tuatha Dé Danann, supernatural beings who could work magic and are the subject of many early Irish tales. When Ireland was invaded by the Gaels, the Tuatha Dé Danann disappeared into another world on the edge of this one. Interestingly, they were also said to have arrived after they were banished from heaven because of their magical knowledge, and they descended on Ireland in a cloud of mist. Right there, you have an entity very close to human supposedly moving from one parallel reality to another and back again. The Sidhe are believed to have the power to influence the human world, and in Irish folklore, they have been blamed for causing many catastrophes.

The Wikipedia entry for the Tuatha Dé Danann is also interesting, starting, "*The Tuath Dé dwell in the Otherworld but interact with humans and the human world. They are associated with ancient passage tombs, such as Brú na Bóinne, which were seen as portals to the Otherworld . . . Much of Irish mythology was recorded by Christian monks, who modified it to an extent. They often depicted the Tuath Dé as kings, queens, and heroes of the distant past who had supernatural powers. Other times they were explained as fallen angels who were neither good nor evil. However, some medieval writers acknowledged that they were gods.*"

The Sidhe, like other fairies, imps, pixies, and other mythological beings, live on the edge of our reality, and that means they know of us and we of them. There are periodic interactions between the two that are captured in tales, myths, and legends everywhere.

Here is a story submitted to me anonymously about fairies.

Liminal People

Back during my childhood, I loved staying at my grandparents' house in Tennessee. I remember their comfy beds, the rocking chair on the porch, and I remember what I would call "the little persons."

I first saw them when I was five or six. The porch backed onto the living room, and from the chair I could see into the kitchen. Hundreds of little people carpeted the floor.

They weren't fairy-like but were just little tiny people. None of them were taller than my fingers. They weren't paranormal in anyway. I knew they weren't good, but they weren't scary. They would surround the rocking chair and sing at me. Even when I got out of the chair and moved about, they still stood around singing.

I saw them for years—and not always at my grandparents' house. Sometimes I saw them at home. People might think I'm crazy—but I swear I saw the "little persons."

Here is another.

I am a retired police officer with over 30 years of law-enforcement service. I am currently an Orthodox Anglican Priest. This encounter happened when I was 14 years old, and my brother was 12.

We were on our way to our grandparents' ranch in Idaho and had stopped off in Mammoth Lakes, CA, to take a rest and get something to eat. After eating, my brother and I went on a hike around the lake. The lake is surrounded by pine trees and hiking trails.

We were walking east on one of trails when we saw a commotion in some bushes south of the trail. We stopped walking and observed a tiny man come out of the bushes, and he turned and *looked at my brother and me. He had a tall red pointed hat and was wearing a blue long-sleeve work type shirt and brown pants and brown knee-high boots. He had a brown work-style belt with a pouch on it. His face was slightly red, and he had a white beard with blue eyes. He looked like a little Santa Claus! I then realized we were looking at a Gnome! He smiled at us and then ran across the trail behind a tree and disappeared. We ran up and searched the area, but we could not find him. We ran back and told our parents what we saw, but they did not believe us.*

I spent that summer researching Gnomes and learned a great deal about them.

Submitted to Weird Darkness and My Haunted Life Too by Dan

If fairies are of interest to you, there is a magnificent book by Margorie Johnson[4] that details many encounters with fairy-like entities. There is an interesting chapter that deals with encounters that take place before or just after sleep or when the experiencer was ill. This demonstrates, she says, that "*certain drugs and gases can affect the vibrations of the human body, and when an anaesthetic is used, it causes the etheric or vital body of the patient to be partially driven out of the physical body, and this makes him or her more sensitive to superphysical vibrations.*" Of the many stories that are recounted in the book, this one stands out to me.

Thomas Shortreed of Galashiels and his son went for a stroll one evening. On the way back, he was surprised to see a troop of figures crossing the road. They were long and tall, moving in a strange way, and there were about twenty of them. They ranged in size, he said, from six feet to about two feet tall. They appeared to just melt into a stone dyke by the road where they vanished. His son saw nothing. Fifty yards or so later he saw another group crossing the road. Again, in this experience, only he saw them, reminiscent of my remarks regarding the Black-Eyed Kids.

If the universe is essentially one of frequency—let's say sound ("In the beginning was the word")—then there will be vibrations across an infinite number of frequencies. All these frequencies exist simultaneously in space—energy in space. Now, if you can recall doing basic physics at school, you may recall playing with water waves and observing interference effects. Can you even begin to imagine how some of these frequencies might interfere with one another and the patterns of waves that may be created? Add to that the effect of resonance whereby things vibrate at higher amplitudes.

According to Wikipedia, *resonance describes the phenomenon of increased amplitude that occurs when the frequency of a periodically applied force (or a Fourier component of it) is equal or close to a natural frequency of the system on which it acts. When an oscillating force is applied at a resonant frequency of a dynamic system, the system will oscillate at a higher amplitude than when the same force is applied at other, non-resonant frequencies.* Imagine this complex, ever-changing universe of vibration.

Now, imagine that you, a conscious being, can only sense a very small range of these vibrations and, in fact, based entirely in that vibrational range. This is your reality in which you, the observer, collapse the waveform—or observe reality around you. In fact, as we said above, you only use a small amount of the information that you are sensing and blot out a lot of it as background and irrelevant noise. You are happily living in this frequency range, oblivious to the fact that the space you and your reality occupies is also occupied by other conscious beings and realities they created on different frequency ranges. In effect, there are parallel worlds filled with beings and realities that are unaware of each other except that sometimes ... there is crossover.

5

CROSSOVER

If my theory is correct and what we are seeing in many of the phenomena discussed in this book is really the crossover of beings from one parallel world or reality into another, then what might the mechanism be that allows this? I think there are possibly multiple mechanisms.

A higher state of consciousness often exposes people to guides and intelligences that speak and help the person hearing and seeing them. As we meditate and pray, we raise our consciousness, and indeed, this is the stated purpose of meditation and spiritual pursuits—to raise the consciousness and, in the words of Rudolf Steiner, to perceive the higher worlds. This pursuit has occupied elements of humanity since time immemorial.

Magicians, alchemists, religious people, and so on have

all sought to scale the heights to the higher worlds, nirvana, heaven, or whatever word you would like to use to describe it. Along the way, these people have been credited with miraculous abilities like walking on water, turning water into wine, changing the weather, conversing with angels, spirits, and even with God himself, becoming immortal, being in two places at once, and having the secret to immortality. You have read many such legends, tales, and scriptures. I documented several such people with short autobiographies in my book, *God's Pretenders*[1], and much can be learned from studying such people.

Entire libraries of techniques to achieve spiritual enlightenment exist, and many more have likely existed in the past. Include here everything from the Bible to treatises on alchemy and magic and everything in between—even some of the self-improvement literature would count. Methods and approaches have been developed that range from fasting and prayer to indulgence in every sinful activity possible and everything in between to gain access to these higher worlds.

Humanity or a part of it, anyway, has given everything in its pursuit of experience of the higher worlds, including willingly sacrificing themselves in its cause. This alone ought to be convincing evidence that there is something of value to be gained and that higher worlds or states of consciousness do exist. All this effort must have been based on the idea that someone somewhere did experience the higher worlds at some time or another. In fact, anyone can and does experience something of the higher worlds in their lifetime. It is inevitable.

On the other side, humanity has been plagued by nightmares and experiences of darkness throughout its existence. These experiences come in the form of all manner of entities that can be best described as belonging to a shadow world of darkness. They come in the form of demons, Black-Eyed people, vampires, werewolves, shadow people, the Old Hag, and many, many more. Throughout history, these boogiemen have preyed on humanity, creating fear of the dark and what it hides and fostering nightmares and paranoia that sometimes resulted in persecution, death, and misery such as that caused by the witch hunts of the 1700s. In fact, experience and fear of these beings and phenomena have often driven humanity to pursue activities designed to enhance spiritual awareness and find the higher worlds of consciousness. There is nothing better to get people to think of heaven than a vision of hell. It is the carrot that has been used by many religious groups in history to scare people into becoming more spiritual!

Meditation, prayer, and psychotic substances like magic mushrooms, LSD, ayahuasca, and other plants have been used throughout history to gain entry to the higher worlds and sometimes to the lower ones—either by accident or design. Researchers like Anthony Peake have investigated how the brain itself produces such substances (DHT) that also appear to provide access to the higher worlds and are part of the dying process.

Peake has written several books about his theories of life after death looking at near-death experiences, in particular postulating that we do not die but rather pass out of time. Indeed, the near-death experience is one phenomenon that has driven humanity's pursuit of higher worlds, and accounts of the experience are commonplace along with the narrative of a massive spiritual change that transforms the person who experienced a near-death.

The idea of using these sorts of practices to expand the consciousness are well known and are taught in many different forms by religions, gurus, magicians, and more. Some of these methods are even used as stated above in self-improvement regimens, and some are used in sports performance. An example of the latter is the use of visualization and imagination where the athlete runs the race in their mind, repeatedly visualizing themselves outperforming.

However, over the last few years, I have concluded that there are many other ways to broaden your awareness and that some of these are not deliberate but accidental. In my little book, *Living Ghosts,* I investigated the ability to be in two places at once (bilocation) and the ability to project the consciousness or even a "ghost" body elsewhere. In that book, I postulated that it was possible for someone to be thinking so hard and deeply about someone or some place that in essence, they put themselves into a trancelike state of mind in which they inadvertently bilocated. I now suspect that being in a certain state of mind can expand our conscious awareness and the frequency bandwidth we are aware of sufficiently to experience strange phenomena.

An example of this is dowsing. In dowsing, as I said at the beginning of the book, one enters a certain state of mind like meditation. Dowsing can involve maintaining this state of mind for long periods or repeatedly entering it in a short space of time. The result is that strange things happen, like finding feathers, having butterflies land and circle you—even in January—and seeing liminal people.

Given a life filled with strange paranormal and magical experiences, as well as having collected and talked to hundreds if not thousands of people about their experiences, I can also suggest that there are certain emotions that can trigger the state of mind required. These obviously include the bliss, peace, happiness, and so on gained via meditation, but I suspect they also involve baser emotions like (in particular) fear along with lust, anxiety, greed, anger, and so on. Fear is, for me, the one that stands out as I began to realize that it was my fear energy or vibration/frequency that attracted ghosts and poltergeist activity into my life.

As I said in *Inner Journeys*, I must have looked like a brightly lit Christmas tree in that other-frequency world filled with the promise of lots of lovely, sustaining fear energy for those entities. In other words, my fear was like a light to a moth. It attracted the very things I feared, increasing the fear "food" and increasing the frequency at which I experienced paranormal events.

I have become totally convinced that entities like the BEK

sense and "feed" on the fear of the victim. I suspect that we have known of this for millennia, and that is where the concept of the vampire originated with a blood lust signifying a need for the life energies of our frequency band. What is life blood but the vibration or energy of our being?

6

LIMINAL PEOPLE

The more I have worked in magic and the paranormal, the more stories and experiences I have collected, and the more research I have done into the quantum world, the more convinced I have become that we do live in an infinite realm of universes populated by beings of different vibrational frequencies. Each group of beings creates its own reality through observation and perception in its frequency range, largely oblivious to the fact that they share the space with many other realities or parallel universes on different frequencies.

It also seems self-evident to me that certain types of entities have an awareness of some of the other realities and know how those other beings can be tapped for energy. Demons, BEK, the Old Hag, and other entities occupy slower frequencies and denser environments than we, but they know that we exist, and some of them know how to interact with us in ways that feed them energies.

For the entities like the BEK and Old Hag, they thrive on the fear that they can create in the right circumstances. Demons play a broader role and understand how to dominate and attach to people in ways that they can live an existence through their host. We call this possession. At the other side of the scale, we have higher-vibrational beings who aspire to help and aid us with guidance, spiritual input, and sometimes, emergency assistance. We call these beings angels and spirit guides. In a sense, all of these are liminal beings.

However, it seems to me that there are human-like beings that exist on the edge of our frequency range, phasing in and out like the two characters I met. They appear like homeless people in some instances and in others, like guardians watching over a particular space or area. I am not sure what these beings are, but they seem to exist just on the boundary of our perception, and when that perception is extended just a little bit, they interact with us in often positive ways. I have wondered if these beings are the recently dead who do not know it, wandering on the edge of reality. Perhaps some are human souls that stay on to help and guide us or to protect the sanctity of place in locations like stone circles.

Here is another example of the sort of liminal person experience I mean.

This story is not my own story, but my aunt's. Recently I was talking to my aunt about my own experiences I have had with the paranormal when she told me a very interesting story that happened to her in 1988. Her story goes like this, back in Winter of 1988 my aunt (Melody) lived in rural southern Indiana. In the Winter the roads would get really bad and be covered in black ice. One afternoon aunt borrowed my grandma's car to take out on a date, because the roads were so bad, and her car was four-wheel-drive. My aunt left, and only a few miles away, she came to one of the large hills that you have to take to get anywhere. She turned down the road when, suddenly, the car went out from her, and she found herself losing control and going into a tail spin. When she stopped the car was stalled and was stuck in the middle of the road. My aunt was okay, but now worried because the car was stuck and not starting, and there she was in the middle of the road, if another car was to come up the hill just then it [wouldn't] be able to stop in time and would hit my aunt. My aunt tried again and again to start her car with no luck.

While she was there trying to once again move the car, light suddenly appeared behind her—it was the headlights of a jeep. Out of the old jeep appeared a tall young man in his early 20s with long blonde hair and dressed in a sort of suit. The thing was, she hadn't heard him approach at all and hadn't seen the lights until that second. He would have had to slam his breaks to stop in time not to hit her, and that should have made a noise no matter what, but there was no warning. He just appeared out of nowhere.

He approached my aunt, not really ever giving her a name but offered to help her. My aunt, just wanting to get to safety out of the road, let him but was skeptical since the car hadn't started for her. He got in the car, and after a minute or so, the car started, and the mystery man slowly drove the car to the side of the road just enough for my aunt to get traction so she could move it. He got out of the car, and my aunt thanked him, surprised at how quickly he'd moved the car and thanked him again for helping her out even if she was a complete stranger. The mystery man said, "It was no problem, you would do the same," and went back to his jeep. My aunt had just got in her car and looked back to see where the mystery man was, but he was gone. He hadn't drove past her, and she didn't even hear his jeep start up and go back down the hill. He had disappeared just like he had appeared from nowhere to nowhere.

My aunt made it home safely that night and continued to think about the mystery man that had probably saved her. After she finished her story, I asked her what she believed him to be, and she said to me that she believes him to be her guardian angel. She said that he knew she was in danger and came to her rescue. I accepted that and agreed, but I also brought up the fact that I know that several people have died on the area of the road, so was it possible that she was visited and saved by the spirit of someone who died in that same area and didn't want to see it happen to someone else.

Either way, whether he was a guardian angel or a spirit, I'd like to believe he saved my aunt that night.

Submitted by Ber Bella to Weird Darkness and My Haunted Life Too

The idea of multiple realities in a single space isn't new, but it certainly starts to explain the paranormal encounters that people experience. It might even be that one of these parallel worlds is where we go when we pass on. It means there are two boundaries where liminal people and entities can exist and be experienced by humanity—a sort of hell and heaven, I suppose.

It also means that we have ways to experience these higher and lower worlds both deliberately and accidentally on the liminal edge of our perception. It means that, given the right set of circumstances, you, too, can engage with liminal entities, be it the BEK or an angelic being. As I always like to say, everyone has a (paranormal) story.

Have you had an experience with a liminal person? If so, please contact me or leave your story at www.myhauntedlifetoo.com to aid me in my research.

ABOUT THE AUTHOR

G. Michael Vasey is a collector of paranormal stories and a magician. He writes paranormal books that will keep you awake at night, poetry that will make you question reality, and books on practical magic, dowsing, and shamanism. He grew up experiencing ghosts and poltergeists and studied and taught magic with a real school of hermetic sciences. These days he can be found in search of the Goddess, dowsing in the forests and mountains of Czechia.

He hosts two popular podcast series. *The The Magical World of G. Michael Vasey* (https://www.spreaker.com/show/the-magical-world-of-g-michael-vasey) looks at reality, magic, and myth, and *My Haunted Life Too* is his vehicle for narrating paranormal stories (https://www.spreaker.com/show/my-haunted-life-too).

He also manages a growing YouTube channel called *G. Michael Vasey—Earth Magic Brno* (https://www.youtube.com/channel/UCejbNlXAbDP8VylIkv2AmUw) where he vlogs about dowsing energy lines, ghosts, weirdness, and more.

He has had numerous paranormal hit books with books like *Chilling Tales of Black-Eyed Kids*, *My Haunted Life Too*, and

Your Haunted Lives. He also touches on magic and the nature of reality with books like *Chasing the Shaman*, *The New You*, *Inner Journeys,* and *The Mystical Hexagram* (penned with Sue Vincent). He likes to splash words on canvas and has issued several volumes of compelling poetry like *The Dilemma of Fatherhood* and *Reflections on Life*. He has also penned two novellas.

Find him at www.garymvasey.com and his blog at https://www.garymvasey.net.

He is currently interested in finding other people in the Brno region to join him in his exploration of the land—www.earthmagicbrno.com

ALSO BY G. MICHAEL VASEY

- **Chasing the Goddess** (ebook, paperback)
- **Chasing Dragons in Moravia** (ebook, paperback)
- **Chasing the Shaman** (ebook, paperback)
- **The Scary Best of My Haunted Life Too** (ebook, paperback, audiobook)
- **Motel Hell** (ebook)
- **G. Michael Vasey's Halloween Vault of Horror** (ebook)
- **The Seduction of the Innocents** (ebook, audiobook, and paperback)
- **The Chilling, True Terror of the Black-Eyed Kids—A Compilation** (paperback, audiobook, and ebook)
- **Poltergeist—The Noisy Ghosts** (ebook)
- **Ghosts of the Living** (ebook)
- **Your Haunted Lives 3—The Black Eyed Kids** (ebook)
- **Lord of the Elements (The Last Observer 2)** (ebook and paperback)
- **True Tales of Haunted Places** (ebook)
- **The Most Haunted Country in the World—The Czech Republic** (ebook, paperback, audiobook)
- **Your Haunted Lives—Revisited** (ebook and audiobook)

- **The Pink Bus** (ebook and audiobook)
- **Ghosts in The Machines** *(ebook and audiobook)*
- **The New You** *(paperback, ebook, and audiobook)*
- **God's Pretenders—Incredible Tales of Magic and Alchemy** *(ebook and audiobook)*
- **My Haunted Life—Extreme Edition** *(paperback, audiobook, and ebook)*
- **My Haunted Life 3** *(audiobook and ebook)*
- **My Haunted Life Too** *(audiobook and ebook)*
- **My Haunted Life** *(ebook and audiobook)*
- **The Last Observer** *(paperback, ebook, and audiobook)*
- **Inner Journeys—Explorations of the Soul** *(paperback and ebook)*

With Sue Vincent

- **The Mystical Hexagram** *(paperback and ebook)*

With Stuart France

- **A Questionable Science—Love and Death in the time of COVID** (ebook and paperback)

Other Poetry Collections

- **Slavic Tales** (ebook and paperback)
- **Reflections on Life: Spiritual Poetry** (ebook and

paperback)
- **The Dilemma of Fatherhood** (ebook)
- **Death on The Beach** *(ebook)*
- **The Art of Science** *(paperback and ebook)*
- **Best Laid Plans and Other Strange Tails** *(paperback and ebook)*
- **Moon Whispers** *(paperback and ebook)*
- **Astral Messages** *(paperback and ebook)*
- **Poems for the Little Room** *(paperback and ebook)*
- **Weird Tales** *(paperback and ebook)*

All of G. Michael's Vasey's books can be obtained from many retailers and book selling sites like Amazon.

NOTES

1. Introduction

1. G. Michael Vasey, *My Haunted Life* (City: William Collins Publishing, 2014).
2. G. Michael Vasey, *The Last Observer* (City: Roundfire Books, 2013).
3. www.myhauntedlifetoo.com

2. Liminal People

1. https://www.youtube.com/channel/UCejbNlXAbDP8VylIkv2AmUw
2. G. Michael Vasey, *Chasing the Shaman* (City: Asteroth's Books, 2020), page number.
3. Stuart France and Sue Vincent, *Giant's Dance* (City: Silent Eye Press, 2021), page numbers.

3. Liminal People in the Paranormal World

1. https://www.medicalnewstoday.com/articles/282217

4. Liminal Beings

1. Thomas Bauerle, *Kanashibari: True Encounters with the Paranormal in Japan* (City: Asteroth's Books, 2017), page numbers.
2. G. Michael Vasey, *Basic Instinct: Erotic Paranormal Contact: The Old Hag and the Mysterious World of Sleep Paralysis* (City: Asteroth's Books, 2018).
3. Gary M. Vasey, *Inner Journeys, Explorations of the Soul* (City: Gary M, Vasey. Thoth Publications, 2005), page numbers.
4. Margorie Johnson, *Seeing Fairies: From the Lost Archives of the Fairy Investigation Society, Authentic Reports of Fairies in Modern Times* (City: Anom-

Notes

alist Books, 2014), page numbers.

5. Crossover

1. God's Pretenders

Made in United States
North Haven, CT
23 November 2024